Y0-CUZ-590

WANDERER FROM THE DELTA

WANDERER FROM THE DELTA

Keith Somerville Dockery McLean

with Deborah C. Fort

Copyright © 2002 by Keith Somerville Dockery McLean with Deborah C. Fort.

Library of Congress Number: 2002096267
ISBN: Hardcover   1-4010-8517-2
           Softcover   1-4010-8516-4

All rights reserved. No part of this book may be reproduced or transmitted in any form or by any means, electronic or mechanical, including photocopying, recording, or by any information storage and retrieval system, without permission in writing from the copyright owner.

This book was printed in the United States of America.

To order additional copies of this book, contact:
Xlibris Corporation
1-888-795-4274
www.Xlibris.com
Orders@Xlibris.com

CONTENTS

Prologue	1
Childhood	25
Youth	39
College	53
Marriage	71
1941–1945—The War Years	87
Back on the Waters	95
Way Back Down in Dixie	107
Timor Mortis	123
Going On	127
Hite Again, Hite Again	137
Twice a Widow	157
Appendixes	165
Appendix 1: The Dockery Daughters	167
Appendix 2: The Grandchildren Set Forth	168

This book is dedicated to the Dockery daughters,
Douglas Dockery Thomas, McKay Dockery Clark, and
Keith Dockery Derbes

And to the memory of my sister
Ashton Somerville Ingram (1917–1985),
who had hoped that Deborah's husband, Ashton's and
my cousin and my godson, Keith Fort,
would write such a book about her life

And to the myriads of friends and relations too numerous to
mention here who have deeply enriched the tapestry of my life

Though we travel the world over to find the beautiful, we must carry it with us, or we find it not.

—*Ralph Waldo Emerson*

ACKNOWLEDGMENTS

Deborah C. Fort, my cousin by marriage and friend by choice, a Washington, D.C.-based freelance writer and editor, with whom I have been sporadically working on this book for the past four years.

William Powell, friend and photographer extraordinaire.

PROLOGUE

I had the usual number of grandfathers but four grandmothers (five, if you count Great-Grandmother Nugent who died in 1930, a bad year for adopted grandmothers).

- Grandmother Shands, my adopted stepgrandmother, the grandmother of my first cousins the Shands girls. She died at about 85, also in 1930, and hers was the first dead body I'd seen.

    I have long used and enjoyed a little gold chair which came from her house 70 years ago.

- Grandmother Nan West, a little bitty old lady. (ca. 1850–1930). She was actually the mother-in-law of my aunt's husband Audley Shands (Eudora Welty loved this kind of tangle). Aunt Eleanor Somerville, a lovely woman who looked like the Duchess of Windsor, married the former Miss West's widower, whose mother-in-law was Nan West, and I adopted Grandmother Nan along with my other grandmothers.

- Grandmother Nugent Somerville (1863?–1952).

Nellie Nugent as a child, ca. 1869

    She was the first woman elected to the Mississippi legislature, and she got every one involved in women's rights, triumphantly voting for the first time in 1923, when I was eight. She was a contemporary of Margaret Sanger, but I don't know if they were acquaintances. She also served on the national board of the Women's Christian Temperance Union (the WCTU) and had the pleasure of seeing Prohibition come in 1919 and the disappointment of watching it go out in 1933.
    Nellie graduated from Martha Washington Women's College in Abingdon, Virginia, in the 1880s.

> Also located in Abingdon is the Barter Theater, where patrons traded chickens, pigs, and other livestock for seats in the theater in the early years of the last century. The college building, still there, has become a beautiful, expensive inn. I went there with Hite McLean[1] in the 1990s.

Great-Grandfather Nugent's letters to my Great-Grandmother, edited by her daughter Aunt Lucy Somerville Howorth (then 82), were published by the University Press of Mississippi as *Dear Nellie* in 1977. Austere, with plain features, Grandmother Somerville never cut her hair, which she wore in a long—eventually grey—braid around her head. She was terribly opinionated, with a one-track mind. She did not put up with trivialities. She was difficult and straitlaced, wanting no one to play bridge on Sundays and seeing dancing as a mortal sin. She was a hard-shelled Methodist (the cliché is hard-shelled Baptist) until the local church began to accept the intermingling of the races; then she took Aunt Eleanor on a four-hour journey to Memphis to the Methodist church there, which was staunchly segregationist. She was the most intolerant person I ever met.

It's lucky she lived when she did. She would probably have founded the White Women's Citizen's Council if she'd lived in the 1960s. It's amazing that she could have been so foresighted about women's rights and so blind to racial inequities.

> Her involvement in political affairs and her determination influenced many of the women in the family who came after her to tread similarly assertive public-spirited paths.

After Grandpapa Somerville's death at 75, Grandmother Somerville built a house in Greenville, 35 miles from Dockery. Later she moved to Cleveland and built a house next door to ours, where she lived for the last 20 years of her life. She was an excellent independent businesswoman. Business, however, bored Mother to tears. Grandmother Somerville had a deformed right hand. The three middle fingers on her right hand grew together, so she wrote left-handed and upside down. My mother was afraid that Ashton and I would be born handicapped.

We never discussed anything real serious with Grandmother Somerville. It was too dangerous.

Aunt Lucy eventually reinvented her mother, turning her into the image of what she wished her mother had been. That her daughter had been active in desegregating the American Association of University Women would not have pleased Grandmother Somerville at all, though probably Lucy's other political and judicial activities would have made her proud.

In the summers, we went to the Tennessee mountains at Monteagle to visit Grandmother Somerville in the old resort that had been ours since the 1880s. There, we were encouraged to improve ourselves by reading the classics and scanning the headlines in the many newspapers that came daily to feed Grandmother's political appetite.

My sister Ashton became engaged to George Ingram on Grandmother Somerville's front porch in 1939.

- Grandmother Louise Douglas Keith Frazier (1860–1942). She was in contrast happy to reflect her husband's dictum., "Give me the luxuries of life, and I'll do without the necessities." She was full of household maxims, including

"The difference between a good and a bad cook is a pound of butter."
"A hole is an accident; a darn is a disgrace."
"One piece of polished silver is an ornament; a wagonload of dirty silver is a scandal."

Grandmother Frazier as a matron.

    We spent summer afternoons with her and Grandfather Frazier in Chattanooga on Glenwood Drive, next to Missionary Ridge. This grandmother was always as fresh as a daisy on those hot afternoons. She powdered her face with chalk on a little piece of suede and always smelled sweet. She would get all dressed up in a freshly laundered cotton or silk dress and go out into the garden to water her flowers. Like us, she loved music and played the piano.

    She was a famous cook, which in those days consisted of having someone else do the dirty work, while the famous cook put on the finishing touches. She made a fresh coconut cake first thing Christmas morning—somebody else grated the coconut, of course. She also made white cakes with many layers of frosting. Ummmmm. Year round, a fruitcake, wrapped in a rag soaked in bourbon whiskey, rested in a hiding place in the sideboard. Very different from Grandmother Somerville!

Grandmother Frazier was an organizer herself in her own way. She was a member of the Colonial Dames, the Daughters of the American Revolution, and the local garden club. Like her daughter, she was into genealogy, and she instructed Mother and Aunt Doots and Uncle Jimmie and Uncle Tommie to refer to "Cousin George Washington, Cousin Thomas Jefferson, Cousin Francis Scott Key, and Cousin John Marshall."

She seemed to deal gracefully with life as a Chattanooga lady after being the wife of a governor in Nashville and a senator in Washington, D.C. According to William Jennings Bryan, "Louise Keith Frazier is not only the most beautiful woman I have met in my travels about the United States, but [also] the wittiest."

Grandfather Robert Briggs Somerville (1850–1925), a widower, surveyed the territory for the first railroad track through the Delta; later it came out to Dockery. Grandfather Somerville, a sweet, gentle man, was married previously to Mary Rutherford Lee in 1879.. Grandmother Somerville never wanted to talk of his first wife.

Grandfather Somerville was an engineer and a mathematician. People said that the records he kept for Engineering Corps of Greenville about the river were the best in the nation.

Grandfather Somerville (late 1870s?).

Grandfather James Beriah Frazier (1856–1937). Granddaddy was governor of Tennessee from 1902 to 1905, a post from which he stepped in 1905 to the U.S. Senate, where he filled out an unexpired term. In both the statehouse and the Senate, he was a strong advocate for public education and for prohibition. He fought against taxes on tobacco and in favor of safeguards for miners.

Grandfather Frazier.

In the Eyes of his Contemporaries

According to his longtime friend and admirer, U.S. Senator Kenneth McKellar, Tennessee newspapers were largely highly sympathetic to Granddaddy's political goals. McKellar quotes the *Jackson Sun* as an example:

> Mr. Frazier is no mincer of matters, and when he gets after the Republican (mal)administration, the fur fairly flies. He is a man of commanding appearance, has a splendid and flowery delivery, and above all is logical in his every utter-

> ance. He took the Republican party by the nape of the neck and wiped the earth up with it; he yanked the trusts around the track until their anatomy was torn to a frazzle; he bored holes in McKinley and imperialism until they looked like a sieve made with a 32-pounder. In fact he did not leave enough of Boss Hanna's crowd and ideas intact even to make a good punching bag for him to work on when he speaks again tonight at the courthouse. (P. 485)
>
> As the *New Yorker* would say, "Hold that metaphor."

Andrew Carnegie (pronounced "Carnaygy"), a friend of my grandparents, told my mother, "Your mother and father are the handsomest couple in Washington," a sentiment echoed by an article in *The Saturday Evening Post*. The Fraziers were also close to Cordell Hull, one of Granddaddy's appointees to political office, and Teddy Roosevelt. Among Mother's friends was Alice Roosevelt, and she was among the guests at Alice's engagement party to Nicholas Longworth.

In 1910, Grandfather Frazier was defeated for reelection to the Senate by a Tennessee political machine headed by Luke Lea. Grandfather Frazier won the popular vote in that election, but lost the vote in the state legislature. After Granddaddy's defeat, Tennessee changed its law, and senators are now elected by popular vote.

Would that the federal government had taken similar steps before the debacle of the election in 2000!

Mother often talked of traveling through Tennessee as Granddaddy campaigned and told us of his popularity among the people. Over six feet tall and stunningly handsome (according to McKellar, Granddaddy was "an Adonis"[2]). Both dignified and approachable, Granddaddy was renowned as an orator and debater. According to a eulogist at his memorial, he combined the virtues of ornate traditional oratory and simple conversational style, often peppered with humor. Over 30 years of observation of politicians speaking at local, state, and national levels led McKellar to say that he had "never heard a convention orator superior to James B. Frazier," continuing, "For the most part, his audience . . . spent a large proportion of the time on their feet, applauding the statements of the orator."[3]

Mother

> When one door closes another door opens; But we so often look so long and so regretfully upon the closed door that we do not see the ones which open for us.
> —*Alexander Graham Bell*

My mother, Keith Frazier Somerville (1888–1978), glossed this maxim as follows: "Something all of us need to remember." She did, and I try to follow her in this optimistic spirit as in many other ways. Mother grew up the elder of two daughters of a prominent political figure. Mother and her sister Louise ("Doots") went to high school at Ward's Seminary (Nashville), a private high school (later Ward Belmont School). Mother then went to the Castle, in Tarrytown, New York. Unlike Doots, who graduated from Randolph Macon (Lynchburg, Virginia), Mother never earned a college degree, something that always saddened her. Still, she inspired deep friendships with her fellow students, some of them lifelong.

When she was 16, Mother was invited to christen the USS Tennessee and immediately formed an organization, the Society of the Sponsors of the United States Navy, at first numbering only 9, now about 600. Most of them (including Mother) christened but one ship, but they often had to travel far to do so. The ships don't come to the sponsors but vice versa, so the young women went to shipyards in places as far flung as Pascagoula, Newport News, Philadelphia, and the California coast. In 1908, Teddy Roosevelt invited the original nine sponsors to the White House for tea.

Soon the growing group was meeting every May in Washington, D.C., with Mother holding many offices—president, secretary, record keeper, for example. She compiled two volumes of statistics and notes on their meetings. By the time Mother was in her 50s, the Sponsors were a big thing. The Secretary of the Navy sometimes showed up at their meetings in the Willard Hotel; once he shared the podium with Mother, resplendent in her big pink hat. Ashton and I were there, shining with her reflected glory.

It was typical of mother that she not only smashed one bottle on the prow of the Tennessee, but also had the creativity to organize smashers for at least a century to come.

Mother christens the USS Tennessee (with her father, Senator Frazier).

It's hard to imagine the absolute void of culture Mother met in 1912 in Cleveland, Mississippi. She came from the hub of Washington D.C., where she met my father, who was secretary to congressman Ben Humphreys and was studying law at nights. She arrived in what felt to her like the boondocks. There wasn't even a library, so she founded one. She once saw a panther walk across the front yard.

Mother had an enormous influence on Ashton and me. Although she did not teach as much tolerance in human relationships as I strive for, she was tolerant racially at times when such fairness was almost never expressed. I remember her saying of how blacks were treated: "It's not right, and it's got to change, and it will."

She had a hot temper.

> *When she went off, she'd sometimes break glasses, just like the tipsy Greeks whom Joe Rice[4] and I would later meet on our travels.*

Sometimes I was angry at her shortcomings. Now I realize that she must have had a really hard time with Mother Somerville, a tyrant, a martinet. Imagine living next to your mother-in-law for the last years of your husband's life and the first five years of your widowhood.

Mother's eye was always on the goal. Whatever goal: to build the library, to plant memorial trees for World War II soldiers, to write letters, diaries, or stories, to teach someone to read, to research her family's genealogy, to get us to college. "Expectation is the limit of destiny," she said, and she really meant what she said. She didn't take time to see the daisies on the side of the road, but that was a conscious choice. Mother expected you to do what you were supposed to do, to discipline yourself, to have a sense of duty, to hew to the moral values. She imbued the need for goals into Ashton and me. But her professional yearnings, like those of her daughter Ashton, went largely unnourished.

WANDERER FROM THE DELTA

1920s Keith and Ashton and Mother.

Half the battle of getting to your goal is to know that you're going to succeed.

From her, I get my love of beauty, flowers, reading, and writing.

Literature is the savior of mankind. That's original with me!

Both Mother and Aunt Doots had a flair for writing; Mother was an aspiring writer. She'd send Will Percy her stories, which he liked and then sent off to publishers but which came back with rejection slips. Mother wrote diaries, notes about trips, and maintained a voluminous correspondence. *Dear Boys*, her letters from Bolivar County to World War II troops in Europe and Japan (published first in the local newspaper and gathered for a posthumous collection in 1991), was just one example.

Mother never put dates on her numerous family trees—"Dates take up too much space." She compiled three major trees—the Keiths, the Somervilles, and the Fraziers—plus Virdie Mullins Hugger's, the Dockerys, the Rices, and ones for other friends. She sold so many trees to American relatives that she was able to travel to Scotland and look up the Keiths there. She knocked on the castle door of the Earl of Kintore, the head of the Keith clan, who was supporting his lifestyle with the money provided by his rich Ohio wife. He was utterly amazed at the depth of her genealogical knowledge.

She also was good at painting and drawing. Had she lived today, her talents would have been nurtured. A watercolor from 1904 survives.

Mother wanted to get through to the light at the end of the tunnel as fast as possible and would push aside everything to reach it. She slapdashed through life to get to her goals. Ashton and I had a creative and bright mother who dreamed up fascinating things for us to do. If she were giving a party, she'd just push everything into closets, not clean up first. (In fact, she never even owned a vacuum cleaner!) It was much more important that the flower arrangements were lovely, and they always were. She took old castoff clothes and turned them into elegant ball gowns.

She loved her "darling husband."

Mother specialized in jonquils. She had 11 different varieties and named each of them. Mother's jonquils were always out for Ashton's birthday in February.

Mother's sister Doots married Uncle John Fort, a beatnik who rarely combed or cut his hair. "Far out" described him. He was a real liberal, doing his own thing on the communist/socialist fringe. He was a published novelist, and he and Doots were friends with some of the important literary figures of the 1920s and 1930s. They had two fine sons, John and Jim, and one late surprise. Their last baby, in 1933, Keith Fort, was going to be a perfect child.

Uncle John was old, however, and money was nonexistent. Neither John nor Doots was arrogant; however, they were totally self-satisfied, and their marriage was the *greatest*—they were best friends as well as lovers.

Doots and Mother were both frustrated writers. Doots did write for *The Chattanooga Times'* society pages, but she had grander ambitions. Doots had a big influence on me. She was a very different kind of role model than Mother, much more open and liberal. Ashton and I loved the Forts' mountain house. We learned to smoke and drink there. Also, the Forts had the wildest books— Hemingway, Fitzgerald, *Stars Fell on Alabama,* lots of other sexy stuff, which they encouraged us to read.

These sound tame in 2002!

As important, they taught us to reach out, to dare.

Father

Robert Nugent Somerville (1886–1946), my father, was a small town country lawyer with a strong sense of equality before the law. He often represented poor people.

He went to Tennessee for a classical high school education at Branton and Hughes Prep School. In 1903, Daddy went to University of Mississippi, where he played football. He was five foot 9 or 10 inches tall, with great big beautiful blue eyes. After graduating from Ole Miss, he went to Washington, D.C. and earned his law degree.

He came back to Mississippi in 1910 and joined Charley Scott's law firm in Rosedale, about 20 miles west on the Mississippi River. Daddy bought a piece of property in Cleveland with two marvelous antique walnut trees on a slight ridge, which he described to my mother as a "hill" (she, knowing Chattanooga, was very disappointed). They built the house on South Leflore[5] in which he lived until he died and she, until it was sold in 1974 when Mother had to enter a long-term care facility.

Robert Nugent Somerville (1938).

 Daddy was gregarious. People adored him just as they do my cousin Jim Fort. Daddy founded the Rotary Club in Cleveland and was the Rotary district governor. (Rotary clubs do a lot of good, providing scholarships for the needy and supporting local charities, as well as being men's lunch clubs.) Daddy was also a proud member of the Phi Delta Theta fraternity at the University of Mississippi (Ole Miss). It was a big thing in Mississippi to be a Phi.

 He doted on his little girls and—like Mother—was supportive and nonjudgmental even when he disagreed with the paths their willful daughters sometimes chose to follow.

 In 1929, on the cusp of the Depression, a teenaged girl drove into him. At 14, I had been driving the Somerville car and was waiting for him to pick up the mail. Before my terrified eyes, he was thrown into the air and landed on the pavement of Main Street. The doctor gave him a too cursory examination and sent him home, but he turned out to have a broken leg and hip, from which he suffered for the rest of his life. His internal injuries were curable in a few weeks, but he spent almost three months in the Campbell's Orthopedic Clinic in Memphis. He was unable to practice law for two years. His expenses were catastrophic, and he sued in a proceeding that turned acrimonious, but still the girl's family's insurance didn't cover the costs of the accident (he had had the financial misfortune to be injured by an uninsured underaged driver).

> *At church in October, 1998, I met a new couple who were just joining up. The wife's mother, my age, was the girl who hit my father 70 years ago. She now lives in Clarksdale.*

Daddy was an altruist and did lots of bartering. He represented blacks and whites alike, and did a good deal of pro bono work for the people of Mound Bayou, a nearby all-black community founded by freed slaves in 1887 and flourishing until the 1920s when a drop in the price of cotton and the migration north started its decline. Fifty pounds of pecans or a country ham or vegetables got you legal advice. Barter was a good idea then, but it just doesn't work anymore. Times were hard. Two years after the accident, Daddy lost money when a bank crashed in Clarksdale and, in addition, when a client paid him in worthless Clarksdale bank stock. But, since no one had money, we didn't miss it. (Or so we tried to believe.)

He and every other Somerville were terribly and justifiably proud of his youngest sister, Lucy Somerville Howorth, who was born in Greenville in 1895 and died in Cleveland in 1997. In between, she was a lawyer, U.S. Commissioner and judge, legislator, and civil rights activist. Aunt Lucy is the subject of a biography by Dorothy Shawhan and Martha Swain (in press).

In the 1920s, Lucy was in law school at Ole Miss when William Falkner [later "Faulkner"] was an undergraduate. She was secretary-treasurer and president of the Marionettes, a thespian group that numbered Faulkner among its members. Standing with Ben Wasson (Faulkner's friend and, later, his agent, Joe's groomsman, and our lifelong friend), she took a play in manuscript from Faulkner's eager hands. Her analysis: "He's a good writer and will make his mark but not as a dramatist."

> Dying at 102, Judge Lucy (Aunt Lucy to us) represented the best of the old school, a great lady. Beloved by all, she had an aura, a personality honed by years of reading, observing, and learning from her profession, her friends, and her surroundings.
>
> In her later years, when we tried to talk her out of her home in Cleveland and into a rest home, she was adamant, "Leave me at home with my books."

While Lucy's money came mostly from retirement and social security, she and her husband Joe Howorth had also invested wisely in Pepsi-Cola stock in the 1950s.

The Dockerys

Joe Rice's father, Mr. William Adkins Dockery (1865–1937), came to Cleveland (founded about 60 years earlier) in the early 1890s. There were nothing but wild trees and swamps on Dockery when young Will graduated from Ole Miss in 1884. His father (no dates available) said, "Here's $100[6], son. Do whatever you want with it." Mr. Dockery got on the train to the Delta, assembled a group of people—probably a few friends and some black laborers who were willing to help them explore the swampland—and homesteaded. At first he rode back and forth the six miles to Cleveland every day attended by a black retainer. He probably paid about $10 per acre. He planted cotton and corn to feed the animals—mules and cows and hogs. Somehow he managed to increase his 10 acres 700-fold. He was an entrepreneur, though that term was not used at that time.

Dockery Farms and the Blues

"I think I heard the Pea Vine whistle when she blowed," sang Charley Patton.

The entrance to Dockery

Frequently, the Delta's sprawling plantations had greater populations than the towns near them. In addition they were also often more economically and socially important; they frequently functioned as self-contained company towns, complete with housing, commissaries, churches, post offices, cemeteries and railroad spurs. (Patton's "Pea Vine" was the railroad that ran from Cleveland to Dockery's Plantation.) Travel was as often from plantation to plantation as it was from town to town. The plantation was the Delta's most important and overarching economic and social structure, an institution that bound black and white Deltans together in a complex web and created the social structures from which the blues grew and the world which it reflects.

Dockery Farms, near Cleveland, was founded at the end of the 19th century when the Delta was still largely frontier. Originally cleared for farming only in its most southern and northern extremities, it was later the home of Charley Patton (the Delta blues' first superstar).

I was delighted to find this painting on the wall of a restaurant in Minneapolis.

Some plantations, including Dockery's, had their own money, plantation "scrip" good only at the plantation store (in our case, in the Commissary). Plantations also often had their own cemeteries, tying their labor force in perpetuity to land many of them had struggled a lifetime to escape.

Dockery script made of bronze and zinc ("brozin")

Where the blues was first performed is problematic, but northwest Mississippi and southeast Arkansas (the Delta) were where the blues was distilled to its essence, and where its emotions and cultural core were the most clearly revealed.

The Delta's untapped resources drew both investment capital and those looking for a new start. Employment drew workers and workers' money drew musicians. This created a frontier economy similar to the boom-time experiences of the Wild West through the availability of capital, cheap land, cheap labor, a valuable product (first timber, then cotton), and convenient access to a ready market.[*]

[*] Much of the material here has been adapted from the web-site of the Delta Blues Museum.

In the spring of 1999, a marker dedicated to Dockery Plantations' role in nurturing blues greats was dedicated.

Dockery today is over 7,000 acres, 6,200 in cultivation.
Like many but by no means all plantation aristocrats, the Dockerys

were good people. Robert Palmer's *Deep Blues* says Will paid his help five dollars a day; the Blues Links (a web-site) agrees that the wage was fair for the time, but says it was 50 cents a day. Both sources agree that Will was an equitable man who did not mistreat his employees.

Mary Nicholson Rice (1832–1937).

Joe's Grandmother Rice voted for Franklin Delano Roosevelt at 100. She came from Charleston, South Carolina. Her first two children died of typhoid fever, and her husband (Dr. Joseph Rice) said, "Let's move." So they went West to Mississippi. They had six more children, Frances Rice Dockery, Nanny Rice, "Aunt Don" Rice, McKay Rice, Sheldon Rice, and Hughla McKay Dockery (Joe's mother).

Dockery.

Joe Rice Dockery January 3, 1906–July 2, 1982

Joe's beloved and beautiful mother Hughla, a school teacher, a church organist, and a loving wife and parent, died suddenly in her early 40s of a cerebral hemorrhage when Joe, the baby of the family, was 14. His sister, Frances, was nine years older. Joe's big brother, Billy, died at age four after a fall out of a Chicago hotel window. Joe, about three, was with the family, perhaps even in the room, when Billy fell. It was a shattering experience.

These deaths had a profound influence on Joe's personality; however, things repressed then today would be endlessly analyzed.

In Joe's childhood, it was "Billy did this, and Billy did that." His mother wanted her dead baby buried in her arms, and her grief-stricken family followed her wishes, although Billy had been dead about a decade when she died in the early 1920s.

KEITH SOMERVILLE DOCKERY MCLEAN

Joe was crazy about his grandmother Rice and his three aunts: Aunt Fannee, Aunt Don, and Miss Nanny (the latter two, spinsters), who reared him after his mother's death. Joe's Uncle Alfred had married Mr. Dockery's sister-in-law Frances Rice. In the 19th century, such intrafamilial matches were not unusual. The opportunities to meet people outside the extended family were much more limited than in later years. Joe was particularly fond of Aunt Fannee and cared for her until her death. For many years, she was wheelchair bound.

Because Dockery was not much of a place to go to school, Joe went to boarding school at 12 or 13. He lived in Bell Buckle (near Nashville), graduating in 1924 from Webb School, which Woodrow Wilson (then president of Princeton) said was the best prep school in the nation. Joe sat on the board of Webb in the 40s and 50s and left the school money.

After high school, Joe got on the train to go to the Wharton School of Finance at the University of Pennsylvania. Also on the train was a contemporary from Memphis, Laurence Cole, on *his* way to Cornell. As they bumped along northwards, Laurence and Joe chatting, Joe decided that he too wanted to go to Cornell, so he just stayed on the train in Philadelphia and went on to Ithaca, New York. He was a good student and athlete and had a tennis scholarship, but Mr. Dockery allowed his son to stay only one year.

Nonetheless, 40 years later, Joe was national president of his fraternity, Chi Phi, for two terms.

Then, Joe's daddy decided that his son was just playing. It was the roaring 20s—bathtub gin, flappers, and the like. Mr. Dockery told Joe to "come on back home" and sent him to Mississippi A&M (later Mississippi State) for a year as a special student to learn about farming.

Joe and his father were not real, real congenial, though they both liked hunting and fishing. They especially had their difficulties when Joe came back from college to help his father farm. Mr. Dockery had been farming for years and years, and he wanted to keep doing things his way—the way that had "always" worked. Joe was young and willful. Understandably, there were clashes.

Joe Rice at the Coronado hotel (California).

Joe never graduated from college, something he always regretted. I think he would have liked to spend all four years at Cornell. He came back to the flood of 1927. I was 13.

Notes

[1] My second husband.
[2] *Tennessee Senators* (Kingsport, TN: Southern Publishers, 1942), p. 483.
[3] P. 483.
[4] My husband to be.
[5] Our street, like nearby Leflore County, was named for Greenwood Leflore, a fascinating, wealthy, prominent 19th- century Native American.
[6] In 2002 dollars, about $1,750.

CHILDHOOD

I was born on May 30, 1914, the cusp of World War I. Geminis often have certain personality traits that don't make us easy to live with—we tend to look in two directions as indicated by our Zodiac sign of twins. This brings on a certain sense of ambivalence but also, I believe, tolerance.

My upbringing was pretty typical of that of little girls back then: "If you can't say something nice, don't say anything at all."

My baby sister, Ashton, a darling blond child two and a half years my junior, was born on February 12, 1917.

My parents weren't disappointed in having only daughters. Although our names sound as if they could be for girls or boys, Ashton Josephine was named for Mother's college roommate. My name, of course, is a long-standing family name. I am Louise Keith. Our names can be changed into Lou and Jo but we never used those potential nicknames. At one point, however, I was "Keithie," and Ashton was occasionally "Ash."

We were reared Methodist and later strayed into Episcopalianism.

Me at about four.

Ashton at two.

KEITH SOMERVILLE DOCKERY MCLEAN

Both Ashton and I were born in Chattanooga, probably in the old house on Oak Street. (Mother "went home" for our births.) During the next 18 summers, we went with Mother back to Tennessee—to see the Frazier grandparents in Chattanooga and to see Grandmother Somerville at Monteagle.

> *Ashton and I had a tempestuous relationship, something that has always saddened me. She said she thought I was better looking, had more boyfriends, had married a man with more money. She was apparently envious of me in her later years, in spite of the fact that George Ingram was everybody's ideal. After her marriage, however, she apparently began to resent our lifestyle—something I wasn't aware of until much later. I guess she thought I had more ... of everything than she, though I remember no friction in childhood. She was such a beautiful little curly-haired blond. (I've always favored curls.)*

We grew up in a wooden house on South Leflore Street built about 1913. The wooden exterior was stained green. (That was Mother's idea, her practical streak—you only have to *stain* once while you have to *paint* frequently.) It was a one-story house with a big screened-off porch in front (actually, every window and door was screened). On the back was a sleeping porch with windows that opened up with screens along two sides. (That's where Aunt Doots stayed when she came to visit.) We slept under mosquito netting in the summers. In the winter, we had a heater. It was cooler on the porch than in the house in the summer.

Mother's room had a small, short four-poster bed where Daddy stayed also for years until, overwhelmed by three females, he built his own room and bath on the back. Mother furnished the house with Mississippi antiques—primitive, simple, clean lines without a lot of elaboration—not like Hepplewhites. (Ashton kept Mother's sugar chest—a treasure—in her dining room in Maine.)

We didn't have our own rooms at first. Ashton and I slept in the middle room. There was one small bathroom. Ashton's bedroom in the middle of the house was dark even though it had two windows facing out on cotton fields.

The pretty living room had a comfortable sofa. Two French doors opened onto the screen porch with a ceiling fan, a great innovation of the 1930s. There was a fireplace, which we used a lot for heat and cheer, and we also had gas heat. Ashton and I were constantly being asked to bring in wood. We often gathered around a Mason and Hamlin grand piano, bought on the installment plan just before the Depression. We three Somerville women all played the piano and sang. Neighbors, who always knew we were home because of the music pealing out, friends, and dates would drop in.

On the beige mantelpiece, Mother painted in black gothic letters Chaucer's blessing, "Here is ye place of resting. Let no swords cross." A portrait of Abram Fulkerson Smith, Nellie Somerville's maternal grandfather who was killed in the Civil War,[1] hung over the mantelpiece. Daddy's rocking chair sat beside a round table with a lamp with one of the first multilevel bulbs. The lamp, which I still use, has a mahogany base and a parchment lampshade. There was also a tall wooden secretary with a drawer; it housed glass treasures and genealogies. Daddy read a lot of biographies—like me today. Mother read lots of Dickens and Scott, as well as the latest books on a huge range of subjects.

Our helper and cook was Charity Bass. Charity belonged to the Daughters of Tabor, an organization of helping women under the direction of either the AME (African Methodist Episcopal) or the Baptist church. The Knights and Daughters of Tabor served much like a hospital auxiliary, going into the hospital in the all-black nearby town of Mount Bayou[2] to comfort and assist the sick within. At church, always wearing white, they sat together and were particularly sensitive to people who were deeply distraught, comforting them actively.

Charity's wages in the early 1930s as I recall were four dollars[3] a week for a five-day week.

> *That was worth more then than now, of course; however, it still doesn't seem enough.*

The small kitchen, not ever as clean as I wished, was Charity's territory. (Mother did none of the cooking except for making coffee and soft-boiled eggs.) On her gas range, Charity produced baked ham, fried chicken, sausages, and ribs, corn bread, black-eyed peas, sweet potatoes, turnip greens with pot liquor on the side. On Sundays, we had waffles with sorghum molasses. Charity worked at a metal-topped kitchen table; we always ate in the dining room. In the back of the kitchen was a bulkhead pantry through which you could walk out on the back porch. In the ceiling of the pantry was a trap door into the attic with inconvenient pull-down steps.

The street in front of the house was the old road to Greenville, which remained unpaved until the 1930s. There was a big yard, always maintained by black people, a series of "yard men," all of whom Mother called "Uncle" until the mid-1930s when she began addressing them by their first names. Some people called their yard men "boy," which was even worse. It shows a lack of interest in another human being not even to know his or her name. One person a day came during the week, and there was always someone on call who made fires, cut grass, weeded flower beds, and planted vegetable and flower gardens. We paid the yard men three or four dollars a week, which would be worth about 10 times that much today.

> *A. P. Henry came to work for me in 1999, about 12 hours a week on the yard. He is a smart, thoughtful, and gentle person and devoted to following my guidance. I call him A. P.*

Mother was a good boss but, unlike Grandmother Frazier, never picked up a shovel. There were lots of flowers—irises, peonies, jonquils, silver moon roses on trellises—and no one was picky about our playing in flower beds. The yard was crossed by a small stream with a bridge, good for water games. My father had a vegetable garden specializing in cantaloupes. We did countless mock wedding ceremonies and made a lot of mud pies—that is how we all got our ideas about cooking.

Ashton and me. (1919)

Growing up in Cleveland, our first cousins the Shands—Eleanette Shands [Leake]; Mary Shands [Hedges], and Dorothy Shands [Martin]—lived within less than a city block of us, and we all became and remained friends. Nearby also were members of the more extended family, including "Uncle Abe" (Abraham Douglas Somerville), who adopted two children, Doug and Joy.

> *Along with other family friends, I spoke at Eleanette's funeral in Fort Myers, Florida, in 1998. We were almost like sisters. We went off to college together. She showed us great courage during her last years. She is my role model for how to die with grace and dignity.*

1917–1918—*World War I*

At four to six years' old, I was not very aware of the Great War. My uncles Tom and Jimmie Frazier were stationed at Ft. Oglethorpe, Georgia, from

1918 to 1920, and Tom went to France. It was the war to end all wars, which of course it didn't. They were in the cavalry corps. Imagine, in 1917, they were running a war on horseback.

Prohibition became law in 1919, but our family was much too busy to care much. For example, since there was no kindergarten in Cleveland, Mother started one in our home, and this was fun for us. As an acquaintance of Andrew Carnegie in her Washington days, she felt that she had a sort of proprietary interest in bringing the printed word to a small town in the Deep South. The library she had founded in 1912 was the seed for what has become the hub of much intellectual life in our community.

> *Today it houses 10 computers and offers training on how to use them.*

Aunt Lucy earned her Ole Miss law degree with highest honors in 1920. She was the second woman to go to law school there, and she was the valedictorian.

We first started going to Chattanooga in the summer when I was a small child. Across the street from the Fraziers lived the Joneses—Caroline and her three brothers, Clarence and Bruce and Arthur. Arthur and I were sitting on a swing, and he kissed my cheek. So I had my first sexual encounter at about seven and promptly ran into the house.

The Joneses were the first to have a radio, an old stand-alone wooden cabinet, which also housed a phonograph. In the early 1920s, almost no one had a radio. We went across the street and listened to crooners like Rudy Vallee sing popular tunes like "Try a Little Tenderness," "Side by Side," and "My Blue Heaven," as well as to political conventions, starting with the race for the presidency between Alfred E. Smith and Herbert Hoover. It was especially exciting to hear breaking political news *live*. In 1928, Alfred E. Smith, the first Catholic to be nominated for the presidency, lost the election when several of the solidly Democratic Southern states went Republican, but Mother, Daddy, and the state of Mississippi voted Democratic.

Mother had a car in the early days of the 1920s. She drove us little girls in an old Dodge from Mississippi to Tennessee, a two-day trip. We spent the night in Northern Alabama, which had a more Northern, less rural feeling to it than did Mississippi.

> *Much later I learned that one reason for this different climate was Alabama's more sophisticated labor force than Mississippi's. There were more educated whites there than uneducated blacks.*

We stayed in country hotels in Alabama and stopped in drugstores, eating toasted cheese sandwiches smashed together and drinking Cokes. In Alabama, we also had picnics—usually chicken salad, cookies, and cheese sandwiches. We'd go wading in streams near Tuscumbia. I remember when we first made the trip, which took about three days at about 45 miles per hour. We always had a Dodge—thanks to Dickens' "Artful Dodger." Mother loved Dickens, and Ashton and I grew up with Little Nell and Fagin.

The Artful Dodger. (1920s)

Once in Tennessee, we split our time between Chattanooga and Monteagle, which were very separate places. In Chattanooga, Grandmother Frazier kept chickens among the flowers in her garden and peach and fig orchards. Monteagle, a WASP Chatauqua community since its inception, was originally Methodist. It's now ecumenical, but the high point of the day remains twilight prayers.

Uncle Jimmie, still unmarried and not yet a congressman, gave us much love and attention. He took us on Sunday afternoon joy rides in his pride and joy, an open, black four-door automobile, which he washed every Saturday morning. Autos were still quite a novelty, and he proudly drove his to and from his office, while Granddaddy took the bus and walked the seven minutes home. Ashton and I especially loved the tunnels around Chattanooga where it was cool in those pre-air-conditioned days. Uncle Jimmie would also take us "over the ridge" or to Lookout or Signal Mountain, where we visited various aunts and uncles and ate lots of watermelon and chocolate cake and drank glass upon glass of lemonade. We'd conclude our expeditions by going downtown to an ice-cream parlor and then usually tour his offices, on the fourth floor of a building with an elevator, which was unusual then.

In later years, Dick Brock, who must have been 16 because he could drive, took me on my first date. His father, Old Senator William E. Brock [I], had been a power in Tennessee politics after Granddaddy was in the Senate. Dick and I and a group of our friends played a lot of croquet. We also often played "Tom Thumb" (miniature golf), which Chattanooga entrepreneur Garnet Carter invented when I was 11. Carter was a big hitter, also opening Rock City on Lookout Mountain, which is still making buckets of money.

> *His nephew Bill Brock [III][4] in the 1960s took national congressional office for Tennessee after Wilkes Thrasher, the Kennedys' heavily financed champion, defeated Uncle Jimmie in the primary, some say by 100 votes, some say by 300. There were reports of voter fraud, which Uncle Jimmie reported to Attorney General Bobby Kennedy, who took no action and*

WANDERER FROM THE DELTA

reportedly said, "Hell, JB, what do you think we went to all that trouble for in your district?" before hanging up.

Immediately after the primary defeat, Bill Brock II came to apologize that his son's entry into the race may have tipped the contest to Thrasher. Uncle Jimmie then threw all his support to Bill III and the family felt vindicated by his subsequent victory over Thrasher as congressman from the third congressional District.

I find Bill Brock an unlikely public figure, but he has been an undeniable GOP presence both in Tennessee and nationally for most of the last 40 years.

The 1920s were exciting times in Chattanooga. In 1925, the Scopes Trial took place about 40 miles away in Dayton. The Fraziers were friends of William Jennings Bryan, who sided with the prosecution. He was a prodigious eater, once breakfasting with Grandfather Frazier. On the other side, Aunt Doots's husband, John Fort, was friendly with Clarence Darrow, who defended Scopes, and H. L. Mencken, who covered the trial. Darrow came to the Forts' house on Lookout Mountain, and Uncle John took Mencken around to see the mountains.

The law that led to Scopes's conviction was not repealed until 1967.

Primary School

We went to grammar school at the largest school in the county, the Cleveland Consolidated School, a three-story building with "rest rooms"—two holers—in the basement. At times, the whole building smelled like sewage. Cleveland Consolidated's three to four hundred students—all white—came both from Cleveland and from the surrounding rural areas. Children were bussed in from all over the mid-Delta, as far as 10 to 15 miles away. The school took care of all precollege grades one through twelve.

Some of the children were desperately poor, almost destitute.

Many ate their lunch of cold fried sweet potatoes in the halls. My best friend, Estelle Myers, and I brought homemade caramel candy, which we gave out during recess.

On the playgrounds were the usual swings and seesaws. There was also a dangerous game called "flying jenny" where kids flew around in circles—There were accidents when kids fell off. We also jumped rope, sometimes tying the rope to a tree. Jumping rope is fabulous exercise.

Daddy bought us exercise bars and rings—he was much more into exercise than mother. We usually walked the one mile to school and took our lunches with us. (When I turned about 10, a boy named Jack Russell carried my books.) We began to drive when we got bigger.

The black children had their own school, and there was a special school for about 50 Orientals (the children of Chinese laborers imported for farm work). Mary Simmons, one of mother's best friends, was the teacher and principal at this school for Asians. Reverend Everson of the First Baptist Church in Cleveland, who had served as a missionary in Asia, also helped out at the school. I knew nothing about the black or Chinese schools except that they existed.

Although I had little sense of diversity then, as a teacher, Mother was deeply aware of the varied ethnic, racial, and national origins of the children in the school.

I leaned more and more to music and practiced endless hours, (sometimes five per day when preparing for the contests which consumed every spring). I can never forget "The Maid with the Flaxen Hair," and I guess it was then that I learned to love Debussy, whose music I still play. My inspiring teacher was Gladys Woodward, such a pretty lady with black curly hair and a persuasive manner, who made her students want to succeed. Music has been one of the motivating drives of my life. I agree with Christian Bovee that "Music is the fourth great need of human beings: first food, then raiment, then shelter, then music" and with this from Plato, "Musical training is a more important instrument than any other because rhythm and harmony find their way into the inner places of the soul."

In 1925, Delta State Teachers College (now Delta State University) was founded in Cleveland. Daddy, Uncle Joe, Aunt Lucy, and Uncle Audley Shands all worked hard and gave generously to make the new college a reality.

We were around 12 or 13 when Daddy taught Ashton and me to drive in our open car with isinglass curtains. We learned during countless journeys in and out of the driveway.

> *When first invented in about 1905, automobiles had three pedals in the floor—a brake pedal, one to shift the gears forward, one backward—and that was how you shifted. Left, back, right, forward. Neutral was in the middle.*

We were a two-car family: One, a Ford; the other, our Dodge. A car cost about $250 (which would be worth about 10 times that much in 2000). Two-car families were rare then, but somehow we managed to keep both cars through the Depression, and Mother always drove to school.

Between 12 and 16, we "dragged Main" on Sunday afternoons. This was Mississippi's version of the Mexican *paseo* where big and small girls would walk in one direction and boys in the other, except, of course, we drove. We were still dressed for Sunday school with patent leather shoes and straw hats, white gloves, and longish dresses, usually cotton pastels.

Ashton and I continued our excellent academic education at Cleveland Consolidated High School.

> *With integration in the 1960s, the schools ignored the changed needs and preparation of the children attending. While we had come to school reading already, many children hitting the system in the 1960s had virtually never seen a book.*

We matured young, perhaps a hangover from the time when

people married at 14 and 15. I entered one beauty contest in high school and lost it.

My father took his little girls everywhere in his black Dodge. When I was 14 and Ashton 12, he started taking us to dances at Ole Miss, which helped us mature socially while we were still young. Daddy was a strict disciplinarian. He taught us to do our duties, which were boring. For example, we had to assist with chores and go to see Grandmother Somerville Sunday afternoons. We also came to his office and typed, filed, ran errands, and posted the mail. That was more fun.

> *If Ashton had been born 20 years later, she would probably have been a lawyer. That would bore me to death, however. Problem with me is I always had my own personal lawyer—Daddy, Granddaddy, Uncle Tommy, Uncle Jimmie, Aunt Lucy, Bill Porteous (who keeps in touch, even after his and Douglas's divorce), Hite McLean, and now Elizabeth Derbes.*

When I was about 10, we went to Chattanooga one Christmas. That was the first time I saw snow. We took the train overnight, which connected to Washington, New York, Philly. It was fun. Ashton and I slept in the upper berths, Mommy and Daddy in the lower ones. We ate in elegant dining cars. I remember rainbow trout. Uncle Jimmie always met the train at 7 AM.

There was no alcohol on the train. In 1917–1918, we were gearing up for Prohibition (1920 to 1933). The temperance afficionados had achieved what they wanted. Grandmother Nellie Somerville was among those delighted.

> *Wouldn't she be furious to learn that red wine in moderation is good for you?*

The Pea Vine railroad in the old days went from plantation to plantation. It was a branch of the Illinois Central Yazoo and the Mississippi Valley—known as the "Y 'n MV—(Boyle to Rosedale to Dockery and back to Boyle). The Pea Vine went from Cleveland to Rosedale on the river with one track out to Dockery. From about 1895 to about 1920, the train ran the entire circuit of 30 miles in about two hours, stopping at all the plantations. The ruins of the depot still remain on Dockery. The Pea Vine went up to get the cotton, which it took to the steamboat on the Sunflower and thence to the Yazoo. It returned with plantation supplies.

The windows went up and down; cinders flew; we sat on wicker seats; a salesman called a "butch" went through the train selling bottled drinks and peanuts.

That's how everyone got around then, not in cyberspace.
They tore up those railroad tracks 25 years ago.
In the new millennium, they are replacing some of them!

Notes

[1] It now hangs at the home of George Mason Ingram IV, Ashton's son.
[2] Mississippi hospitals were segregated until the mid-1970s; sick whites went to the Cleveland Hospital, where their emotional needs were tended by white volunteers. Blacks, of course, were welcome to do menial labor in both facilities.
[3] This would be worth about $40 in today's dollars.
[4] William Emerson Brock, III, a U.S. representative from Tennessee (1963–1970) and one of our U.S. senators (1971–1977), after his defeat became Ronald Reagan's secretary of labor (1985–1987). He was later chairman of the Republican National Committee (1977–1981) and U.S. trade representative (1981–1985), running unsuccessfully for the Senate from Maryland in 1994 but making a ceremonial entrance into the Republican National Convention in 2000.

YOUTH

The first big happening in my young life was the "27 Over-flow"—a big flood of the Mississippi River. As Ashton and I walked to school in April, the levee broke at Scott, the site of the Delta and Pine Land Company, an enormously successful English syndicate, which owned some 25,000 acres of Mississippi in the 1920s, and 38,000 by the 1940s. This firm introduced farming with up-to-date methods based on scientific research—leveling, irrigation, rotation of crops, genetic research on seeds, and the like.

Now Delta and Pine retains only about 1,000 acres, just enough land to do research. It is involved in genetic seed development of all crops—soybeans, wheat, corn, cotton. You can plant pink- or blue-tinted cotton and, more important, insect-resistant seeds. A planned merger with Monsanto went awry in 1999, and Delta and Pine sued Monsanto for something over 27 million dollars; however, they are still collaborating on genetic mutations. The new owner, Prudential Life Insurance, sold the conglomerate in 1999 for 18 million dollars to a private citizen from Southern Missouri.

Delta and Pine land rents for $100 per acre—sells for $1,000—about twice as much as ours brought in 2000.[1]

The Overflow was frightening—the water stopped only seven miles southwest of Cleveland. A wall of water inundated the land west of town. The only thing we could see above the water was the elevated railroad 12 miles to the South. There was a heavy break ("boil") in the levee, and people piled sandbags on the levees to control the water, but the water broke through, knocking everything to one side. Father took Mother, Ashton, and me on a train trip on the elevated track which ran down to Greenville. Someone criticized him later for using the flood to entertain us, but he correctly thought the trip was educational and historically important.

From the train windows, we could see that there were six to eight feet of water all the way to Leland. Joe was boatman for Senator Leroy Percy during the flood. He drove a motorboat into the Percy's house in Greenville and tied it up to the newel post and lived with the family on the second floor. In an oral history years later, Joe Rice told an interviewer from Mississippi State that he remembered vividly retrieving corpses from up on the levee, which he then had no choice but to throw out into the river. What a shattering experience! Joe also said that when he was returning from Greenville up the Sunflower in his boat, he realized that night was falling, and he took shelter in a cottage by the river. The blacks who lived there took him in, fed him, and gave him the best bed in the house. He kept in touch with them.

In Greenville, people in low areas went up on levees and camped. Hoover made a big splash (so to speak) for his presidential aspirations when he sent the Red Cross in to rescue and feed the refugees. Senator LeRoy Percy overruled his son William Alexander's wish to send the Delta's marooned blacks to Vicksburg, which stayed dry, and they were put up on the levee to live or, in many cases, more accurately, to die.

The blacks weren't voting in those days, so what *they* thought of Hoover remains unknown, but white Mississippi voted against him in the next election.

Two years after the Overflow, in 1929, the stock market crashed. We had nothing to start with, so what could we lose? The financial situation affected every phase of American life, although we, laughing, said that no one had any money, so no one missed it. (That's not true, of course, but one simply did not buy anything except necessities.) A big weekend evening's entertainment was making pull candy or playing bridge on someone's front porch. Lots of longtime friendships and a few love affairs developed under the ceiling fan over a game of auction bridge.

If I sound nostalgic, perhaps that is pardonable in this age of instant gratification and the flow of cash into material things.

Mother started to work in 1929, teaching kindergarten and first grade for 10 years to help Daddy send us to college. She was a popular teacher and taught many kids not only to read but also to love beauty. It was hard work, but she loved it. Mother made many friends among her students, who for years would come back to tell her, "Miss Keith, you taught me to read." How she did it all is more than I know—running our home, working, tending her sick husband, trying to make ends meet, and staying up late at nights sewing up old dresses to make us party clothes or sometimes just to clothe us.

I had a big crush on a high-school classmate, Billy Thomas, when I was 12.

Joe and I were introduced at a dance in Rosedale when I was about 14. My father had already brought me out to meet Mr. Will Dockery. The Dockerys had horses which they let a friend and me ride. I didn't ride sidesaddle, though Joe thought I should. I was not a very good sportswoman, although I had been riding—English saddle—since I went to high school. Later on, Joe had horses named Sunny and Paint, and a hostler to groom, feed, and exercise them.

Before we had air-conditioning, we took a big tub of water, floated in it a 50-pound chunk of ice, and put it in front of an electric fan turned as high as possible. One block would last the evening at dances, dropping the temperature from above 100 degrees to 80 degrees. The ice was stored in sawdust in underground ice houses. Only rarely did we have this apparatus at home. It was a big deal.

I didn't *really* start reading seriously until I was about 15. We had a wonderful education: Cleveland High was an excellent school, with four years of Latin and two, of science. Our English teacher, the famous Effie Glassco, who wrote a weekly column for the *Bolivar Commercial* reporting on the doings of local bigwigs offering her unique world view, was my inspiration and role model.

> ## Effie Glassco Through the Decades: A Tribute
>
> Effie Glassco taught Ashton and me in the 1920s; she was still going strong 40-plus years later. While our daughters had fled the black Sunflower County schools to Memphis, other students were receiving the same kind of riveting and astonishing education we received decades earlier. One of her students from the class of 1959 published a tribute in 2001, which reads in part,
>
>> Every high school has its most memorable teacher, the topic of tales tall and otherwise at reunion after reunion. Effie Glassco was ours. Catholic school kids can tell "Sister Caligula" stories, but they pale in comparison to our public school accounts of Mrs. Glassco.
>>
>> She may have been short and reedy, but she used a fierce temperament to tower over the lunkiest farm boy, the toughest jock in her class. No one crossed Effie Glassco and lived to brag about it.
>>
>> She reserved a special wrath for school administrators. Effie Glassco never met a principal or superintendent for whom she had anything but contempt. There were days when she would spend an entire class period regaling us with her opinions of the latest madness the administration had conjured up. She directed one especially vitriolic tirade at a principal who distributed a memo touting an "almost unique" opportunity. "There's no such thing," she said. "It's like being almost pregnant."
>>
>> But if she didn't suffer fools gladly—or at all—she had an intense passion for the English language, for good writing and for students who could write. Defying the conventional wisdom at the time as well as the fiats of principal after principal, she separated her students by

skill level, teaching classes ranging from college-level English composition to remedial reading.

Those of us she allowed to ascend to the Olympus of her top-level class found the first year or so of college English was a dreary review of the material she had forced us to learn. You did it her way.

If anything—football practice, a school play, cheerleader tryouts, or, in my case, the school newspaper—got in the way of class work, Mrs. Glassco would aim her sharpest weapon at you: a withering ridicule that could reduce the biggest, strongest and meanest of us to tears. Many days I could have slithered from her class under the door.

Her heroes were writers. She told us of Wirt Williams, a fellow Cleveland High alumnus whose novels received two Pulitzer Prize nominations. One became the movie "ADA," which starred Susan Hayward and Dean Martin.

She introduced us to the poetry of William Alexander Percy, a plantation owner just down the road in Greenville who was one of the South's literary icons. Percy, a Renaissance man if there ever was one, was equally at home in the cotton fields or in a tony literary salon. He adopted his young nephew, Walker Percy, who was later to become one of the nation's literary giants.

She led us into the twin worlds of glamor and decadence in F. Scott Fitzgerald's books while teaching us to work our way through William Faulkner's long, convoluted sentences. A reading list for Effie's class could range from "BEOWULF" to Thomas Wolfe, tossed with a soupcon of Shakespeare's sonnets.

We were in class one day when a school office proctor came to tell Mrs. Glassco she had an important telephone call. She dismissed the young girl with a wave of her hand and told her to take a message.

"We're talking about Shakespeare," Mrs. Glassco said. "I can't be disturbed."

> A few minutes later the girl came back and told the glaring teacher that the principal said the call was very important and she really should take it. Cleaning her glasses with a thumb and forefinger (a characteristic gesture we never could figure out), she stormed down the hall. A few minutes later she returned, positively radiant.
>
> "Guess who that was, children?" she said. "Tyrone Power."
>
> The actor, who had married one of Effie's students, called from Hollywood to invite her to visit them for the weekend and share their suite at The Peabody when he came to Memphis, 100 miles up the road, where he was to appear in a play.
>
> The next week, we heard every detail of the visit, down to her count of the shoes in his closet.[*]
>
> [*] Quoted with permission from Bill Givens, "Effie And The Power Of Words," *Memphis Commercial Appeal* (March 12, 2001).

In Mrs. Glassco's English courses, we read Sir Walter Scott's *Ivanhoe* and *Kenilworth* and Shakespeare's *Macbeth*, *Hamlet*, *The Taming of the Shrew*, and *The Merchant of Venice*.

Another fine teacher, Catherine Ward, often directed Ashton in school plays. A traveling company did Shakespearean plays at the high school auditorium for students and people from across Bolivar County. Among others, we saw *The Merchant of Venice*, *Hamlet*, and *The Taming of the Shrew* (I still love *Kiss Me Kate*).

The sciences were a little bit weak, and, like many girls then, I was told that I was not good at math, and I stopped at plane geometry.

> *I could have gone as far as I wanted, and now I know I'd have loved to study economics and business.*

Cleveland high school gave us a terrific classical education, but one that didn't lead to earning money. While we girls were expected to grow up and have a family, Daddy wanted us to be prepared to make a living, so that we wouldn't become totally dependent upon a man in case we were divorced or widowed. Then, however, about all a woman could aspire to professionally was to be a stewardess, a nurse, or a teacher.

I had no debut myself—we didn't have debuts in the Delta during the Depression. In addition, neither Ashton nor I needed them. We started going to dances at 14. There were no dancing classes, but everyone, boys and girls alike, took music. Somehow, I knew how to dance just as I knew how to walk.

> *Joe and I were both good dancers. We danced through our years together. I especially remember the gorgeous, sparkling evenings on transatlantic crossings.*
>
> *I remember one last dance with Hite on the boat coming back from South America, but he was getting a little short of breath then. He couldn't twirl as fast as he used to.*

In spite of the Depression, the 1930s were frivolous. We lived for the Saturday-night dances. These were of two sorts: private by-invitation-only parties and script dances, which cost five dollars a couple and drew several hundred people. The money collected paid the orchestra about $250 and rented the American Legion halls where the balls took place. We danced to the music of some wonderful jazz bands, including a white band, the Mississippians from Ole Miss, and a black one, the Redtops.

> *The Redtops also played at Douglas's debut a couple of decades later.*

The special dance was the last, usually "Let Me Call You Sweetheart."

Ready to dance.

We went in groups, not on individual dates. Somebody's mother was the chaperone. We'd get home about 4 AM. Usually we double dated—three boys, two girls, and a mother or father. *We didn't drink anything stronger than Coca-Cola, although maybe the boys had some alcohol*

The Percy boys, Walker, LeRoy, and Billups Phinesy (Finn) were always at the dances, as was Shelby Foote. I was the older woman (they were closer to Ashton's age than mine, being from two to seven years my junior). All of us remained friends through the years. We were always in the same group with the Percy children, and our parents were friends. Under the reigning class system, we all went to the same churches, regional meetings, country clubs, schools, and—eventually—belonged to the same fraternities and sororities.

Sarah Farish Percy (LeRoy's wife) had a niece who was a good friend of "Baby Keith's" in college. Roy Percy's wife, a heart surgeon who lives in Winston Salem, is also a friend of hers. Friendships are like a woven tapestry.

KEITH SOMERVILLE DOCKERY MCLEAN

I graduated from high school as salutatorian on my 18th birthday. Among the members of my wonderful class with whom I remained close are Saralie Walker Heard, Estelle Myers Bedwell, and Eleanette Shands Leake. I always feel a certain warmth when I run into one of the 30-some people who were in our class of 1932. Though I fondly remember a classmate named Tom Hyer from Cleveland, most of our beaux were from other towns.

I had reddish-black hair in my youth.

I've never colored my hair, going swiftly grey at about 60 and staying there.

Here I am during my high school years sitting in our garden on a swing Mother designed.

A Fairy Godmother

In the early 1930s, I first visited Ashton's and my benefactress, a lovely lady named Letitia Pate Whitehead Evans. She was a Coca-Cola heiress, whose late husband had been Grandfather Frazier's law partner. Later, she took Ashton and me on wonderful trips and had us visit her on her estate in a big Greek revival house on a hill in Hot Springs, Virginia (then as now, a stylish resort, spa, and riding center for the wealthy). Those trips were eye openers, voyages to another world, which deeply enriched our lives.

Our fairy godmother.

Keith Somerville Dockery McLean

Emmie Whitehead, Prince George Romanov, and me.

Inside the Hot Springs house was a large, illuminated globe. Mrs. Evans and her tweedy, charming second husband, Kelly, a retired Canadian colonel, had a lovely Steinway, which she played for fun. Every night, there were formal candlelit dinners set with lavender, green, or yellow tablecloths and Czechoslovakian crystal wine glasses and lovely china. Fresh flowers, arranged by an impecunious niece, graced the table. Every morning we had breakfast in bed served by a uniformed French maid.

> *In 1994, I visited the site and found only the deteriorated shell of the house with a little piece of Italian marble standing inside. It should have been made into a museum, but now it was for sale for $350,000. Mrs. Evans left it to the Episcopal Church, and just off its grounds is a little chapel. We looked in on a service, and the priest and four others beckoned us into the choir. There we celebrated communion with the assembled parishioners.*

Mrs. Evans, a high-society philanthropist, was generous, gracious, and well-read among Southern writers as well as in the English classics. Ashton and I went to visit Mrs. Evans frequently—usually separately because of schedule conflicts.

(Mrs. Evans family had had the Coca-Cola bottling rights for Europe since about 1910 or 1912.) Her first husband, Joe Whitehead, who had been Granddaddy Frazier's law partner and one of two founders of Coca-Cola, tried to talk Grandaddy into putting $500 into Coca-Cola, but Grandaddy turned him down, either predicting that "no one is ever going to drink that stuff" or because, as a strict Methodist, he found the caffeine in it—to say nothing of the cocaine—immoral, or both. For whatever reason, the sad fact is that he did *not* invest in "Coke," period.

Mr. Whitehead died when I was small. When I was in my 20s, their two sons were in their 40s. Both had already married and divorced several times, and both died young of the same rare kidney disease.

Although money could not buy their sons' happiness, the Whiteheads/Evans did much good with their money. Mrs. Evans was comfortable and generous with her wealth. She gave ambulances to the British in World War II, money to the Episcopal church, and a surgical pavilion to Emory University in Atlanta in 1930. In addition, she endowed a nursing home in Richmond—the list goes on and on.

"Great wealth," I remember her saying, "is not an unmitigated blessing."

I'm not sure I agree. In any case, it is a powerful tool.

Mrs. Evans, who was rather portly, would send us boxes of discarded designer clothes—Balmain, Chanel, Balenciaga—which Mother would ingeniously redesign into evening dresses for her slender daughters. Once, Mother made over a dress of brown chiffon with patterned silk, trimming it in Mrs. Evans's castoff mink.

The Evanses had money in the 1930s on Bill Gates's scale and, like him, they were wonderfully generous.

Note

[1] Recent Delta and Pine data courtesy of Leroy Percy, Walker Percy's brother.

COLLEGE

In the fall of 1932, Eleanette Shands and I boarded the night train for New Orleans where we enrolled at Sophie Newcomb College. Those were two wonderful years with new friends in our Pi Beta Phi sorority. Both of us had several beaux in the Tulane Med School, and we met lots of wonderful people in the New Orleans community (many have remained lifelong friends). New Orleans was exhilarating after my limited, small-town background. I was thrust into a cultural life featuring concerts, plays at Le Petit Theatre, Gilbert and Sullivan operettas, art shows at Newcomb, and debut parties. I loved spending my freshman and sophomore years in a big city like New Orleans with its access to music and culture in general.

We lived in dorms—mine was the Josephine Louise house, a three-story brick with a smoking room in the basement. You could smoke, and we all did, anywhere off campus or in the smoking room. Eleanette was my roommate the first year. The next year, I had two or three different ones, a couple of whom I've kept up with.

1933—Prohibition Ends, FDR Inaugurated

Daddy didn't like Eleanor Roosevelt, but Mother thought her wonderful.

A lot of our orientation towards university life was affected by the reality that *nobody* had any money. We relied for entertainment on our personalities and exchanges of ideas. For instance, we listened to the radio, which was free, and, in general, we lived more simply than we do today.

There was a 10:30 curfew five nights a week. Friday and Saturday, it was 1 or 1:30. When you left the dorm, you signed out, saying where you were going and with whom.

Eleanette's Aunt Mabel was socially prominent and offered an invaluable entrée into exclusive societies like those of New Orleans or Charleston. She got us invitations to swim at country clubs and to Mardi Gras balls. Louisiana's "closed" society wasn't closed to me! It was a social swirl!

> *Society was stultified in the 1930s; it hadn't changed by the 1950s. There were fixed rules. The women all went to the balls together, while the men were in Krewes (clubs) with names like "Proteus," "Comus," "Rex," etc. Joe was in Comus and Mystic, whose queen was a married lady. No one from outside of New Orleans could be queen. The Mardi Gras theme in one year in the 1950s was 18th century Peru, and the costumes were gorgeous. Mine was pink and deeper rose with big puffy organdy sleeves. It still hangs in my storage closet, and I wore it to the Mardi Gras celebration in Merigold in 2002.*

If you didn't have a call out—"Miss Somerville, Miss Somerville"—you felt awful, and sometimes that happened over and over again. Sometimes I'd sit for hours and only dance three or four times all evening. If you did get a call out, a member of the Krewe would serve as go between and escort you to the man who'd asked for the dance. Your partners gave you favors like little satin bags to hang over your shoulders, little silver boxes, or junk jewelry.

Sororities had *some* serious purposes. They held bake sales to support arts and crafts schools, for example. We started the Arrowcraft, a craft school on the Tennessee border. Staff brought in mountain people who made crafts for money—hand-woven mats, towels, etc—and taught them to read on the side. We also helped people who were less privileged, giving toys at Christmas, doing charity work in New Orleans. In fact, we were salving our consciences about having too much.

> *At least we didn't have way too much then, as we do today.*

Jack Russell from Cleveland, my first male best friend who had carried my books home from grammar school, was now in medical school at Tulane. Jack introduced me to the medical crowd, which sponsored dances with full orchestras. At Newcomb, I had a big crush on M. L. Michel, a real, real attractive man from an old New Orleans family, who went on to practice medicine there. We sat together and held hands on the porch of the Josephine Louise house at Newcomb.

I love South Texas. Texans flocked to New Orleans because it was prestigious to go to Tulane Medical School, and parents of Texas girls frequently sent them to New Orleans for college—away, but not too far. Ditto the boys. I took up with Walter "Hondo" Meyer from Hondo, Texas, near San Antonio, a good-looking medical student who looked like today's TV political analyst and historian Michael Bechloss. There was plenty of sexual attraction between us; we both loved to dance and were good at it; I enjoyed his friends. Hondo and I ("Slim" Somerville was *my* nickname) were serious, going together two to three years, and keeping in touch after I left Newcomb.

Hondo's father was a country doctor with a very primitive office. Once after Hondo had earned his MD, I visited out there overnight and went on a house call with Hondo. He was tending to Mexicans in a shack in a poverty stricken area. I sat in the car and waited until Hondo came out.

> *When Kay was at del Rio in 1965, I passed on a bus through Hondo. A woman there knew what had happened to the Meyers. Hondo and his parents had died, but his sister and brother were still there.*

WANDERER FROM THE DELTA

I studied music and practiced, not nearly as much as I might have with the competition from too many other diversions. In music appreciation, which met at the civilized hour of 11:30 AM, I learned about Wagner's *Ring* and studied Rimsky-Korsakov's Scherherazade suite and learned to play Mussorgsky's *Pictures at Exhibition.*

In college, I was more interested in things social than in academic learning, with a grade point of 80 at Newcomb and 84 at Ole Miss. I studied enough to get a degree in applied piano, which was supposed to lead to teaching. I managed to pass most classes; however, I struggled with the freshman English survey with Miss Stone—it was so hard—and one spring my sophomore literature grade did nor quite make the mark!

> *Both Hite and I flunked our sophomore literature courses, an odd prelude for lifelong readers.*
> *I have always begun my days by reading in bed, while drinking tea or coffee.*

I had a terrible time with French, which I squeaked by with a 76. I didn't ever crack a book that second year.

While I was studying and partying, Joe was over here at Dockery, farming with his father. I sometimes saw him in Cleveland over school vacations, and he came to New Orleans once or twice when I was at Newcomb. He rarely set foot on the Ole Miss campus because of its rivalry with his "alma mater" Mississippi State.

I also visited Newcomb friends. One of them was Pimmie Spencer from San Antonio, Texas, who turned out to be one of my best lifelong friends.

> *Pimmie is a free spirit, good golfer, and avid traveler who had five children and then had her teeth straightened. We've kept in touch and are still close.*

After the summer was over, I took what was called a "condition exam," successfully erasing my D in literature and moved on to Ole Miss that fall of 1934.

That same year, Ashton registered there as a freshman (the family could not afford to send the two of us to a private college at the same time). Tuition was about $500 per year.[1] Times were still hard, but no one seemed much bothered. Ashton and I would cash a $5 check at the beginning of the month and divide it for our allowance to cover movies, stamps, ink, other odds and ends. Cigarettes were five cents a pack, and we all smoked.

Ole Miss had 500 students then

—None of them black—

and we knew them all. Fraternity and gym dances consumed every weekend, and we had a great time. Daddy had lots of close cousins in Oxford—Somervilles, Bishops, Howorths, and Culleys—and they added greatly to our enjoyment. Daddy was a strong fraternity man and had a wide acquaintance among the alumni and the boys who knew him as "Mr. Bob." The Phis, including G. Hite McLean and his brother Lee, were particular friends of Ashton's and mine.

There was definitely a financial depression in the 1930s—but no depression for me! I was gay and flighty then.

We were not very serious students, but I fondly remember how the telescope in Dr. Kennon's astronomy class helped me see the beauty of the stars even more intensely than I had just looking up on late summer nights.

The Barnard Observatory, where the class was held, was fully restored in 1992. It now houses the Center for the Study of Southern Culture.

I became enamored of the Episcopal Church at Ole Miss. Episcopalians were more open, less dogmatic than Methodists. Dr. Edward McCrady, who was rector at St. Peter's in Oxford, became head of the University of the South (Sewanee). His sermons were philosophical and intellectually stimulating; his liberalism contributed to mine. He took up questions of science and religion. Episcopalianism at Ole Miss, while deeply spiritual, was more intellectual than the Methodism of my childhood. In both churches, at different times, I sang alto in the choir.

The gym dances at fraternities were more exclusive—Daddy gave us an entrée—than the dances at Miss Ella Somerville's Tea-Hound, a local dance hall and restaurant. Miss Ella, a cousin of Daddy's in Oxford, was a well-read friend of Faulkner's. A big lady with dark hair, so popular and so attractive, she was a member of Delta Gamma sorority founded at Ole Miss. Stark Young, who wrote *So Red the Rose* (a hit in the 1930s) may have had a romance with her. She was the town doyenne, and her charcoal-broiled steaks at the Tea-Hound were famous. Her white frame house, set up on a knoll, was long and low with one big room where fraternities gave dinner dances on Saturday and Sunday nights.

I went to the Tea-Hound with several dates, including my great friend, Hite McLean. Hite, who was in love with his future wife of 42 years, Lenore Kimbrough, thought I was in love with A. G. Bowen, who was, however, only a wonderful, wonderful friend. The head of the English Department was David Bishop, the grandfather of all the Howorths and the father of my friend Vassar. Mother had known him when she went to Texas to see cousins just after the turn of the century—an ambitious journey highly unusual for a young girl at that time.

> In the 1940s, Miss Ella made the Tea-Hound into a successful dress shop. She left her house and a whole stack of first editions of William Faulkner to Vassar Bishop, a niece, who was also a member of our crowd.

Those were exciting times at Ole Miss. I had three roommates, all English majors. For two wonderful years, the four of us danced, studied a bit (I mostly practiced piano), and played lots and lots of bridge. One of my roommates, Genevieve McBee, ran away to Memphis to get married secretly to William Barbour, a ceremony solemnized with the dime-store ring I lent her. I attended the official wedding at Christmastime in Greenwood, Mississippi (the only one most people, including their parents, knew about).

KEITH SOMERVILLE DOCKERY MCLEAN

> *Genevieve and I remained close (she and William settled in Yazoo City) until she died, tragically young, of cancer.*

I continue to see another roommate, Erin Gwin Lail (now in Jackson), frequently. At one point, Joe dated my third roommate, Jessie Smith, a smart beauty who also died young.

I didn't read much contemporary literature until the end of college. I found *Sanctuary* extremely boring. I began to read Faulkner when *Light in August* came out in 1932, and I enjoyed his last book, *The Reivers*.

Faulkner was living in Oxford when I was at Ole Miss in 1935 and 1936. In those days, so many of the literati, including Mother, were really down on Faulkner. "We don't associate with those people," I remember her saying, "Why should we have to read about them?" I met Faulkner once when his stepdaughter Cho-Cho Franklin, a member of Ashton's sorority, held a Chi Omega style show at Rowan Oaks, his Oxford home (now a museum). By the time Cho-Cho was a senior, I had graduated. Faulkner, a small and very gracious man, walked down the steps and formally greeted Cho-Cho's guests. There was an aura around him . . . . He was somehow glamorous in a tweedy English sort of way.

> *They tore down the old post office, his "postage stamp" of earth. He famously incompetently, ran the post office. I own a souvenir brick from the building.*

I spent the second semester of my senior year at Louisiana State University in Baton Rouge, where my piano teacher, a French lady named Madame Shafner, inspired me greatly, and I spent two to three hours a day practicing. Thanks to my diligence and my wonderful teachers, I won first place three times in competitions held by the Mississippi Federation of Musicians.

> *The piano challenges memory three ways:*
> *You need visual memory to read the notes on the page.*

You need muscular memory in your hands and arms.
And you need auditory memory.

I also took *boring* education courses at LSU. I somehow made it through my senior year and then doubled back to Ole Miss to receive my Bachelor of Music degree one June day in 1936 in the Grove, the hub of the campus.

In 1936, Ashton went to Louisana State University where she studied under Robert Penn Warren, who inspired her deeply even though he persistently called her "Mr. Somerville." Among others, she was dating one of Daddy's Phi boys from our Cleveland and Oxford days.

Ashton (1939).

My oil portrait by Karl Larsson. (1940)

In a letter to the Mississippi State alumni magazine, Joe Rice offered to replace a dead bulldog, "Ptolemy," as the team's mascot if the Maroons beat Army in 1936. They did, and Bully I, a handsome brown dog with a black mask, was the first in a long line of Bullys culminating with Bully the XVIII. Joe took Bully I on the train to West Point and gave him to Mississippi State's coach, Major Sassy. After Bully I was killed by a bus, he was solemnly interred at the 50-yard line.

I didn't mind Joe's dogs, which always lived outside, though I developed a fear of them after my oldest granddaughter Carolyn almost lost a finger to one in the 1960s.

Halcyon Days

Immediately after graduation in 1936, I went to San Antonio to be in Pimmie and Bob Tucker's June wedding as a bridesmaid.

Pimmie's wedding was almost as eventful for me as for her. I was having such a good time that I stayed on for three weeks, even though the bride and groom had long since departed by train for their New Orleans honeymoon. While in San Antonio, I managed to break up with my then inamorato, Hondo. We had had some fine times together, but ended up being incompatible. He was much more interested in things scientific; I, in things artistic. The end of the affair was inevitable. Writing finis to that chapter left me free to pursue other things.

Besides, I had fallen for the best man, Terry Geddis, who became a superintendent of schools in San Diego. Like many of my favorite beaux, Terry was athletic, tall, dark, and good-looking. He was seven or eight years older than I was, and I *thought* he saw me just as a good friend. There *were* lots of friends there for the wedding.

I remember a train trip one night in 1936 when, coming back from a Memphis wedding in which I had participated, somebody came on the train waving a newspaper—

Not a radio, not a TV, not the Internet. A newspaper!—

and shouting that the Duke of Windsor was resigning "to marry the woman I love." This was a great scandale!

After Ole Miss and Pimmie's wedding, I spent a lazy summer in Cleveland playing bridge, swimming in the Sunflower River and at Denton's milk-processing plant's swimming pool, which was open to the "public" (meaning, actually, the Dentons' friends), and sunbathing.

. . . *Gainful Employment*

In the fall, I took my only paying job, teaching music in Ackerman, Mississippi, in Choctaw County, traveling from the Delta to Ackerman on the C&G Railroad (the Columbus and Greenville "Come and Go"), a short train with three coaches and a freight car that ran across Mississippi, stopping almost everywhere—or so it seemed.

Lifestyles in the hills differs radically from those of the Delta. I lived in a boarding house run by Miss Lula Potts. Her meals were wonderful.

We'd call it "soul food" now.

Communal living with strangers proved difficult, however. My roommate and I were incompatible, and I did not like the narrow-minded bigot who was superintendent.

His treatment of me would now be called "harassment."

My salary was $60 per month, plus the income from my 12 private piano students, who paid $4 per month. Room and board was $25. I hated the job a lot, but I hated the social scene and my living conditions even more.

Reading *Gone with the Wind* was the highlight of my year! There were some happy weekends visiting Mississippi State, Ole Miss, Memphis, anywhere but Ackerman.

Mother had loved teaching, but I found it ghastly, and I was glad to quit in the spring.

Home Again, Off Again

Joe and I began to ride horseback together and then to attend football games in New Orleans and Baton Rouge. When we started dating, Nashville's Rachel Burch Willmot, a social butterfly, fox hunter, famous cook, and homespun philosopher, advised Joe, "The shortest route to the lady's boudoir is down the aisle of a church." Eventually, he listened.

When Joe was away, the Christmas before we were married, Terry Geddis hopped a bus from San Diego for four days to spend the holidays with me. I had thought we were just good friends, but apparently he had more than that in mind . . . . Marjorie Francioni, another friend from LSU, visited us for Christmas, and Ashton was home from Baton Rouge. We had a grand Christmas, and then Terry went back to California, Ashton and Marjorie back to school, and Joe returned from his Arizona trip with matrimony in mind.

After my graduation from Ole Miss and year's purgatory in Ackerman, Mrs. Evans invited me to visit her that fall in Hot Springs, Virginia. When one visited there, it was like a dream: such a wonderful large home, servants at your beck and call, parties and dances and entertainment around the clock. In October and November, the socialites converged upon Hot Springs, so I met many exciting persons, including Grace Vanderbilt, the widow of Cornelius, who had a mansion nearby (Mrs. Evans told me once that the only problem she had with me was that I did not use a broad *A*. That set all spoke with a Virginia accent which sounds sort of British: r*ah*spberry, tom*ah*to, etc.). A wonderful Russian gentleman and his very foreign daughter were among our friends. Between parties, he gave me piano lessons, and I practiced lots on Mrs. Evans's fine instrument. She urged me to let her send me to Juilliard, but I did not take her up on that. Again I was having too much fun. One of my chief motivations during those years was just that—having fun—not a bad idea even today. Grandmother Somerville always thought we were frivolous, and she may have been right.

At about this time, "Mrs. Evans" became "Letitia" to me.

When she had to attend a Coca-Cola board meeting in Wilmington, she took me along for company. It was pretty amazing for a woman, even one who held huge amounts of stock, to sit on such a powerful board. Letitia probably owned half the company and held all the bottling rights for Europe. I met and dined with the members of that board, including its attractive, generous chair, Bob Woodruff, a great admirer of Letitia's. Next, we went on to New York, where we stayed for 10 days at the luxurious Savoy Plaza Hotel. Grace Vanderbilt, who had come a long way from her birthplace in Loudon, Tennessee, entertained us and 10 other guests for dinner at her mansion at 640 Fifth Avenue. Eight liveried footmen attended us. I was about half the age of the other guests. Everything was lavish. The food, accompanied by several fine wines, was beautiful and delectable. The house was truly a museum.

> *It is now a modest, blocky, newish building with a chic discount store headquartered in Scandinavia on the street level.*

I entertained on the piano afterward. I should have been frightened but recall only being exhilarated. I remember playing one of Liszt's *Études* and his *Liebesträume* and ending with a dashing rendition of *Malagueña*.

Later that week, because Letitia had friends involved, we attended the National Horse Show at Madison Square Garden. I especially loved the international jumping events, and I still do. Nonetheless, I skipped out on the horses one night and went out on the town with Sonny Russell, a friend from Oxford, Mississippi. We visited some friends of his near Columbia University, where he was in school, and finally went dancing on the Astor roof.

> *Sonny told me in 1991 that that night had cost him a month's salary! Was it worth that? I doubt it, but he wasn't complaining.*

Letitia took me shopping and introduced me to Bergdorf Goodman for the first time. We bought *two* suits, some very fancy high-heeled, ankle-strap platform shoes, and other accessories. I was in heaven. The year after I finished college (1937), I had a couple of beaux and a couple of romances. For example, I met the Russian prince George Romanov, a direct descendant of "Uncle Nicky" Romanov—the last czar, who was murdered by communists. The prince and I became good friends and went to New York together both by car and train. A chauffeur traveled after us. We were very circumspect. Eventually our paths parted, and that was the end of my affair with royalty.

Letitia was terribly disappointed that I did not choose to marry the Russian prince whom she had picked out for me. I might have been a czarina—well, not quite, since his uncle had been deposed in the 1917 revolution. The prince was a handsome fellow and a nice person but not quite right for me to settle on for life. (Between the wars, many Russian nobles came to America and became "floorwalkers" [sort of upscale security guards] in Saks in New York and Palm Beach. In that role, they hobnobbed with the likes of the Duke of Windsor and Wallis Simpson.)

In the early days of Joe's and my courtship, he would call me on the phone *long distance*—Mother and I thought that was so wonderful. (He even called me from *Mexico,* where he spent many of the winters of the 1930s.)

I turned down the Evans' offer to send me to Juilliard, when a telegram came from Dockery to Hot Springs: "WHAT'S KEEPING YOU UP THERE STOP COME HOME STOP JOE RICE." Bowing to the inevitable, when I got ready to come home in the fall, Letitia gave me a three-carat Cartier diamond ring from Paris, which I now mostly keep locked up. (She gave Ashton a similar ring.)

After going to Washington to see the Howorths, I respected Joe's appeal and did come home. An extremely well-dressed me stopped off in Washington, D.C., to visit Aunt Lucy, who was there on the Board of Appeals of the Veteran's Administration, one of several posts to which she was appointed by FDR.

I stayed with the Howorths at their Kennedy-Warren apartment on Connecticut Avenue. Their apartment was unpretentious, and I slept on a pull-down bed in the living room. People said that both Aunt Eleanor (Shands), who was also visiting, and I looked like the Duchess of Windsor. At least, we wore our dark hair the same way parted down the middle and smooth. Aunt Eleanor, widowed in 1936, never remarried. There were grand times at numerous Washington cocktail parties (my drink of choice, thanks to Letitia's mentoring, was an applejack cocktail). Two gatherings were especially memorable: one in Aunt Lucy and Uncle Joe Howorth's living room (my bed safely tucked in the wall) and a bigger one in the fall of 1937 for Eleanor at a downstairs ballroom. An avid reader and book collector, Aunt Lucy helped to enhance my love of literature. One of the books she gave me was inscribed "To Keith because you love words."

Lucy and Joe were in Washington from 1934 to 1957. After that, they both went to Cleveland to practice law. Much earlier, in 1923, Lucy had been in the Mississippi legislature.

Back in the Delta

Shortly after Joe's return from his latest Mexican business trip, he and I realized that we wanted to marry. I got a great letter from Hite, when my engagement to Joe was announced. "Well this is the last time," Hite promised, "that I'll ask you for a date!"

Mississippi Alpha of
Phi Delta Theta

University, Miss.
February 22, 1938

Dear Palsie,

I want you to know that our romance has ended, and I don't want you to expect me to ask you for another date, ever again. I'm plenty mad about this matter, and am afraid that the strings holding our love lives together have been broken. I hope that we can be friends, but no more dates.

I want you also to know that my heart is broken. Experienced as I am in this line – the lady-friend-marrying-off-on-me-stuff, I still have a heart no matter how battle scarred it is, and this has put a new scar on it, or rather it will be – its still in the wound stage now. I am getting the jump on the fates in the beautiful affair which I am now having; the young lady was married before I started going with her. For all I know though, she might have heard of my reputation, and thought that was the quickest way to get started again. What am I anyway, a man or a marriage bureau? Woe is me.

Thanks for the shock-absorber. The minute I got it I started in remembering the good times we used to have. I would certainly love to come down and help youall celebrate, but you know how devilish it is to try to get to the Delta from here. If there is any way possible, though, to make it down, rest assured I'll be there to see you off. I am looking forward to meeting the new mate, and am sure that he is a right guy, because you and I generally had the same ideas as to right guys.

The picture in the Commercial was good. I wish I kept memoirs, that would certainly go amongst em.

Among other things, I'd certainly love to see your mother go into action in the next few weeks. Be sure to tell her to settle down for me, and to watbh out for those Kools, or she'll run a hot box.

Tell Mr. Bob that Billy Hix has finally lined us up with the head political machine on the campus, or rather, lined up a political machine, with himself as the head of it, and that's the truth. We ought to go strong in the next election. I suppose you know that I'm living at the house, and it is really swell.

As ever,

Hit

Never Say Never Again, Again.

WANDERER FROM THE DELTA

Forty-seven years later, he was proved a liar.

Joe gave me a black Packard for an engagement present. He also gave me a gorgeous diamond and ruby ring which had been his mother's and which I still treasure.

By 1937, Hodding Carter's newspaper the Greenville *Star* merged into the *Delta Democrat Times,* which Carter, who was active very early in the Civil Rights movement, quickly transformed into one of the South's most courageous papers.

> *This brave editor began laying the foundations for his greatest contribution: the 1960s crusade against segregation and racial discrimination in the state, a policy as controversial as the Percys' anti-Klan struggle of the 1920s. In 1946, Hodding Carter won a Pulitzer Prize for his editorials against racial and religious bigotry. His wife, Betty Werlein Carter, my lifelong friend, was a literary oracle. Betty did a lot of Hodding's research.*[2]

Ashton graduated from LSU, specializing in theater and "histrionics"—acting, dramatics, and public speaking.

> *Later, she went on to portray Tallulah Bankhead in* Tallulah *in the Little Theater at Norris, Tennessee. After George and she moved to Fairfax in the 1950s and early 1960s, she acted in a number of little theater roles.*

Death Is So Much Around These Days . . .

Will Dockery died in 1937 of lung disease at Johns Hopkins. He was 72.

That same year, at 80, Grandfather Frazier just went to sleep after his Easter Sunday nap. Mother, who worshipped her father, had had a presentiment about his death. She was at tea in Grandmother Somerville's house, felt ill, and ran to her home next door. As she burst through the house, Uncle Jimmie's phone call announced that Grandfather had just died. She always thought he'd first stopped by to say goodbye.

> *My, that each of us could wish for such an easy transition to the world beyond.*

Death is a part of life even as a river flows into the sea.[3]

> "What do you think it will be like over there? Sleep?
> "Oblivion—At least that's what I hope."

The Duino Elegies—*I read them almost daily like a Bible—better than a Bible for me. My favorites are 1, 5, 6, and 10.*

> . . . We, who have always thought of happiness as rising, would feel the emotion that almost overwhelms us whenever a happy thing falls.[4]

There's been a big celebration for a woman of 105 in Cleveland. One of her ancestors was a town founder. Last year, she was really angry to still be here. This year she seemed better, however. I hope everybody after 100 has a quiet, peaceful death, that she (or he) just goes to sleep and does not wake up.

I think I realized I was mortal at about 10 when I saw Grandmother Shands's dead body. It didn't really get into my head, however, until I was an adult. When Mother was lying in the living room in her casket, I heard my grandchildren Will Porteous and Elizabeth and Louise Derbes whispering together. One of the little girls said, "I can't believe she's dead." "We know she's dead," explained Will (about age seven), "because she's not talking."

We are all going to die. When you lose someone, however, the loss is permanent, though it slowly gets easier to bear. I've tried, however, to teach my girls Rilke's calm lesson.

True as I believe that is, so is the epigram Bill Ferris, the founder of the Center for the Study of Southern Culture, quotes: "When an old man dies, a library burns to the ground."

I don't think I'm going to heaven; I don't think I'm going to hell either; I don't think I'm going anywhere. I therefore dread dying.

An afterlife? I doubt it, but could we go through all this for nothing?

Notes

[1] It would be worth over 10 times that much now.
[2] News commentator (and Jimmy Carter's press secretary) Hodding Carter III is their son.
[3] Kahlil Gabran, *The Prophet.*
[4] Ranier Maria Rilke, *The Duino Elegies,* trans. Stephen Mitchell (New York: Vintage, 1992), lines 110-114.

MARRIAGE

The Wedding March, 1938

I married Joe Rice Dockery, a complex man about nine years older than I.

> *Joe and I always had independent agendas, but we did many many things together. Usually, we agreed.*

Our small wedding took place in the Methodist church in Cleveland decorated for the occasion with California ferns. Ashton was my maid of honor, and the attendants were my cousins Eleanette Shands and Joy Somerville. They wore floor-length, electric-blue dresses and carried white tulips and roses. I wore my Grandmother Frazier's antique brocaded satin dress, remade for the occasion by our dressmaker, Mrs. Champion, who also made everything in my trousseau, and the Keith veil, which had been worn by all the brides in our family for three generations.

Joe's best man was Count Renato Caselli, a local man whose mother had married an Italian count who was part of the Italian court of Victor Emmanuel III (the "Little King"). Renato was certainly not little. He was six feet tall. Joe's groomsmen were Ben Wasson and Gwin Shelby, a longtime friend of my family.

> Ben remained a close friend of ours until his and Joe's deaths in 1982, and we frequently met the Casellis in Europe in the 1950s and later.

My aunt Margaret Dolan Frazier arranged all the decorations and flowers. There were lots of parties around town. Our reception at the Women's Club featured fruit punch and a cake designed by Grandmother Frazier. She had invented cake pans that wedged inward to make a perfect circle.

> Ours was the same circle of cake five feet in diameter that we used for Kay's, Douglas's, Keith's, and Carolyn Clark's weddings.

There's a wedding photo of me but not of Joe—grooms didn't always figure in wedding pictures in the 1930s. Too bad—Joe was a handsome groom, even with the flu he brought to the ceremony. Many people, including my Russian prince, sent telegrams of congratulation, all of which Mother collected in the wedding book she made for us.

My wedding photo.

Joe Rice

Joe Rice Dockery had a great deal of vision and understanding. (He was just "Joe" to me but often "Joe Rice" when I was talking about him.) He was highly motivated and very much able to take hold of an opportunity and make a lot of it. Yes, he was, like most of us, self-centered. He was certainly self-motivated.... To succeed, he didn't mind projecting himself, and his vision was inclusive and broad. He was a big man in many ways: Literally, he was six feet plus like his daddy, and figuratively, in his ambition, drive, and intensity.

Joe was an avid reader and a smart businessman with lots of friends. At first interested mostly in business, sports, travel, and social events, later Joe began to discover his great intellectual curiosity. Joe was something of a dandy, a generous one, however. He'd buy lots of clothes and give them away.

The government was looking for someone to head up Civil Air Patrol to search for lost planes—private and public—and Joe did it. As a volunteer, he got to know upper echelon military stationed nearby. Joe donated his private plane and pilot to the war effort for a number of years. With General Spattz ("Tooey"), famous in World War II as head of the Air Force in England, Joe and I also went duck and goose hunting. We'd meet on Saturdays and go up in a private plane with pilot Bill Chapell, who lived at Dockery and who was also our cattleman. His wife, a seamstress, helped me alter all my girls' clothes.

I took flying lessons for a couple of years, but I never soloed. Joe never took lessons or flew his own plane, figuring—as usual—that if he could get anyone to do something for him, so be it. Both Douglas and Kay also took flying lessons. We would all handle the plane when we were airborne. It had a life of its own—air currents pushing it up, down, sideways, upside down. We all learned to do this roll thing. When a plane goes into a spin, you need to raise the nose to straighten out. In the warm months, we looked down on brown and green and tones of yellow. The river went flowing through extensive timber stands of primeval oak, cypress, sycamore, and sweet gum trees. Everything was gray and brown during the winter, but still beautiful.

Joe helped to reorganize the New Orleans Cotton Exchange, hanging a copy of the Degas painting of the subject in the Dockery business office, and started the National Rice Council in Houston in the mid-1960s. (We raised rice for the first time in 1947.) As president of the Rice Council for about six years, Joe got to know millers, growers, and government people. He was a real good executive on the cutting edge of the farming scene. Once, he got heavy into cattle, and we had beautiful pastures. One of Joe's many good ideas: If you want to learn about something, go to an expert.

I did the same thing when I had to manage the plantation, after Joe's death in 1982. For a dozen years, I was a farmer.

That's something Joe and I had in common—we both reached out to new experiences and people—travel, civic affairs, outside interests.

I wish I could get one of my men back—either one would be fine. Both Joe and Hite became more intellectual as they aged. They were both wonderful husbands in completely different ways. In both cases, our intellectual compatibility was profound.

That Joe had no college degree did not stop him from being a voluminous and eclectic reader. His prep school education grounded him in Ovid and Shakespeare, and he also read contemporary literature like Michener, historical novels, and business journals.

While Joe was something of an absentee father—he *was* gone a lot—he often took one or all of us along on his trips. I remember a glorious Christmas trip to New York City when the girls were about four, six, and eight. And, vacations permitting, they spent quite a lot of time with us on our yacht. Joe tried to teach his daughters worthwhile skills, including swimming, horseback riding, and tennis. He was an understanding person, caring for the girls and for me; however, all families including ours have their ups and downs, but unlike in today's world of quick divorces ... we rode them out.

We each did a lot of things together. And a lot of things apart.

Joe had drive and ambition. He wanted to be the best: the best swimmer, the best tennis player, the best everything.

Honeymoon

After the wedding, Joe and I took the last ferry across the river at Greenville and spent the night at Lake Village where the hotel keeper had arranged a little bowl of lavender wisteria on the table. It was a bit tacky because wisteria doesn't keep well, but I fondly remember the champagne. Then we left for Texas.

What does one do on a honeymoon?

We made love and slept.

We didn't exercise.

And

We read.
We wrote thank you notes.
We went sightseeing.
We walked on beaches.
We swam and sunbathed, swathed in coconut oil.
We made friends.

We drove all the way to Acapulco after stopping for a night in San Antonio to see Pimmie and Bob Tucker and their baby son Robert. Next, we headed for Mexico. Joe had already developed a lifelong love affair with everything Hispanic—Mexico, Spain, Portugal, Central America. He spoke and read Spanish well, while I had only tourist Spanish. Later, we both read James Michener's *Iberia*. The Pan American Highway was being built, and many spots were all but impassable with gigantic boulders in the roads.

Joe's Lincoln Zephyr, a red convertible that made quite a splash in 1930s Mexico, however, always managed to limp through. Adorable Mexican children begged, "Wash your car, Meester?"

On our honeymoon, we went to many places in Mexico from glamorous Acapulco to fishing villages. Acapulco was and is so beautiful. We spent mornings on Caleta beach for sunbathing, swimming, and drinking the milk through straws poking out of coconuts; afternoons, we often went to another beach—"Hornos" (ovens)—for more of the same. We also went deep-sea fishing and enjoyed wonderful seafood meals on the open terrace of our hotel, El Mirador, with the waves of the dark blue Pacific Ocean breaking below us. At El Mirador, owned by our friend Don Carlos Bernard, we watched divers plunge 50 or 60 feet into the ocean. At night (then and now as well), they carried flambeaux, dropping them as they dove.

We went sightseeing at another beach called *"Pie de la Cuesta"* (Foot of the Hill) and watched the 15-to-20 foot waves that came in from the Pacific ocean. Only experts could surf in them.

It was thrilling, and we were happy.

We were in Monterey on our honeymoon on March 20, the day after the Mexican government took over the nation's oil.

> *Joe was always dabbling in oil from the 1930s until the end of his life. He was talking to me about oil on his deathbed.*

Green Years of Marriage—1938–1941

Returning home, we moved into Dockery, bringing our lovely wedding presents, my housekeeping inexperience, and our shared enthusiasm for our new life together. From the very beginning of our life together there, our friends and helpers Robert Whittington, who ran the Dockery Service Center, and his lovely wife Flossie made life easy and wonderful for us. Eventually their daughter Mary Amelia became a fast friend of our daughters.

We fixed up the old house, putting in a 75-foot by 35-foot swimming pool in 1946.

> *Since then, I've wished we'd been more modest. The upkeep is steep.*

On an average weekday at Dockery, I went swimming before breakfast. Next, I'd read for a while, before we ate the breakfast someone else had prepared. After breakfast, Joe would go down to his office, and I would go on errands—marketing, getting the car serviced, picking up odds and ends, and the like. I'd also participate in civic organizations, like women's clubs and Episcopal church groups.

Both of us came home for lunch, which was soul food—cornbread, turnip greens, and the like—again courtesy of the cook. Until it became untenable for a young married couple to share quarters with an old man, Uncle Tom Adkins lived with us, moving out finally after a *long* couple of years. His lunch always included an iced-tea-sized glass of buttermilk.

From 1934 to 1942, Joe was on the Mississippi Board of Corrections. The prison owned about 10,000 acres of prime farmland, which the Board helped manage.

In the afternoons, Joe and Uncle Tom went back to the office, and I read, wrote letters, planned menus, worked on the gardens, took walks, sewed, practiced about an hour a day on the Steinway Joe gave me, provisioned Dockery, and visited with friends and relatives, most importantly my parents and Ashton, while she was still living in Cleveland. I loved sewing so much that I often got up at 5 AM to get the machine going.

Many late afternoons, Joe and I took a leisurely hour-long horseback ride around Dockery. At night, we played tennis and bridge with neighbors Shelby Foote, Will and Walker Percy, the Payne boys, and Billy Wynne and his wife. She compiled a cookbook made up entirely of her cook's recipes. We also used to play poker. I wasn't much good at that. Nighttime gatherings always included sing-alongs around my Steinway, with me, Ashton, or Mother at the keyboard. We had a couple dinners a season for friends at Dockery. We also went out of town frequently on weekends.

We tried to keep up our literary connections. Someone organized a great-books club; someone else organized a short-lived vintage film group on Tuesday nights—things like *Ben Hur,* classic Italian films, Shakespeare.

Religion

Joe grew up a Baptist, I, a Methodist. Both of us became Episcopalians, and Joe read the whole New Testament in English, then in Spanish. Religion in the South is a social as well as spiritual institution.

> *My church has the best "coffee hour" in town. (That is, cheap-white-wine or Cokes* or *coffee hour.) Everyone stands around and talks. I also enjoy our "saints and sinners" dinners. There's also an altruistic motive. The Episcopal church gives me a feeling of anchorage to basic principles beyond me, myself, and* I. *We try to help the less fortunate. The Bishops Fund for World Relief is just a drop in the bucket, but every drop counts.*
>
> *Whether people are or are not worshipers is not important to me. Intellectually and socially, I am a much better person when I go regularly to church. I am more secure, have a better outlook, am more able to accept the losses and deaths that come almost daily. The church is a wonderful influence: If you're an Episcopalian you're never never not at home. You're never alone . . . "And also with you . . . " says the* Prayer Book.
>
> *I am one of those unorthodox persons who considers herself a Christian. I don't endorse* all *Christian tenets, but I am a better person for worshiping communally. Everything about Christianity is not good. Take the Inquisition, for example, or Henry VIII who gets credit for divorce, but all those wives' heads rolled! Shocking!*
>
> *Denominations split off and throw stones at each other.*
>
> *I don't believe in original sin. I don't believe in an afterlife.*
>
> *I think of God, whoever or wherever he is, not as a person but as an act.*

Keith Somerville Dockery McLean

"God is a verb, not a noun," *according to R. Buckminster Fuller. He's right.*

* * *

I went to several black funerals, but not until I was grown. The black people would put their arms around your shoulder and tell you, "It's OK, cry as much as you want." At one funeral, someone called on me to say something about "the deceased." I said platitudes, platitudes from the heart.

White-robed ushers come to the really grief-stricken and hug them. This is a long-standing tradition that continues. It probably originated with the Methodists or the Baptists, but now there are also ushers in the black Roman Catholic churches as well as the evangelical sects. The blacks dress up for church fit to kill—suits, jewelry, high heels. Besides wailing and ushers, choirs sing, sometimes to the beat of a drum, gospel music like "Amazing Grace" and "Onward Christian Soldiers."

There's only one black member of my Episcopalian church today, and she is as faithful as anyone else. I'm confident that any communicant of any color would be welcome. Churches are still segregated in practice though not in theory: Blacks come to our funerals, and we go to theirs. We have a way of including each other: "We'll see you at the funeral." This means a lot to all of us.

I once heard a story about a Mrs. Fisackely, who said to her maid, "Now that things are changing here, and we are all coming together, I wish you'd go to church with me."

Said her maid, "Oh I love you so much, Mrs. Fisackely. I'd do anything for you, but I sure don't want to go to church with you."

The Quiet Pleasures

Flowers and music are as essential as oxygen for me and have been since I was a child. You are never so close to God as when you are in the garden. While my helper and I always plant a few vegetables like spinach, we plant roses, roses, roses. You can't have too many roses. They give such pleasure with their long blooming season from April or May into early November. The Delta soil is so rich.

Mother was influential in the landscaping at Dockery. She laid out formal gardens at Dockery based on Pierre L'Enfant's 1820 designs for Elmwood in East Tennessee (Athens) for Great-Great-Grandmother Sarah Ann Penelope Fore Keith (the wife of Alexander Keith).

With plenty of help, we copied Mother's plan. For years, we had an elaborate formal garden, but recently that has become a burden because of invasive plants. There's a big circle in the middle with cape jasmine and beds for annuals and perennials. (The dimensions are the same as the tennis court—120 feet by 35 feet.) Huge. We have Mississippi iris and other spring bulbs—tulips and daffodils—and flowering shrubs. One rose bed, about 20 years old, is full of hybrid tea roses. Roses are right expensive—$15 or more per bush. Our main specialty in summer is zinnias—red, yellow, blue, chartreuse, pink, and lavender. Gardening is an endless well of inspiration. Digging in the compost heap impresses me with the beauty of Mississippi soil.

In my flower arranging, Mother was again a role model.

At Work . . .

Joe gave me a piece of land in 1940, right before he went to join the war effort—about 800 acres in Tunica County, about 60 miles away from Dockery toward Memphis. Joe paid $30 per acre ($300 in 2002 dollars); it's now worth about $1,000 per acre. I think he wanted me to have my own personal income, and he was right. It's been wonderful. My farm mostly raises cotton; it was farmed first by Van Morgan, a black man, then by Francis Boyd, then by his son Mike. The Boyds are white.

> When Van died in the 1950s, Joe and I went to his funeral in a black country church just off the farm. Van was buried in a tiny cemetery on the farm. These acres make up a major part of my estate.

Joe made a lot of money in cotton seed futures. When you farm, your whole life is within its parameters—growing things out of the earth, adding chemicals and nutrients, planting and picking, rotating crops, drainage and irrigation (too much rain, not enough rain).

> We shut down the cotton gin (invented in the late 18th century) at Dockery in the mid-1960s when people began to use gins cooperatively. Cotton was picked here by hand until the 1940s, when mechanized processing came in.

Joe had oil holdings in Arkansas, where I now hold some stock, and in Oklahoma. There were wells in land he owned in a South Mississippi pasture and near the little town of Port Gibson, but they petered out after about a week. As a Dockery well came in, so it went out: It didn't pay to drill. (You had to restore the land back exactly as was according to 1940s environmental contracts.)

And At Play

After Joe and I were married, we frequently went riding in groups. We went fox hunting (but there was no shooting—the hounds grabbed the fox eventually). Though I never attempted jumping, Joe was expert, winning many trophies. I quit after two falls and three babies during the 1940s. Joe was disappointed but understood my feelings. The hunts were fun, and on them we met many interesting people in Mississippi, Tennessee, and Kentucky.

> Later, we also went wild-boar hunting in France.

I continued my piano studies, now with Mary Catherine Gerard, a fine pianist, teacher, and friend, who eventually also taught Douglas to play.

We returned many times to Mexico after our honeymoon, and twice Joe and I studied *español intensivo* in San Miguel de Allende, a small colonial town in the mountains about 125 miles northwest of Mexico City with the only Gothic cathedral in Mexico. Among our real good friends were a far-flung group of expatriates in Taxco and Cuernavaca. The scene must have been like Florence or Paris in the 1920s. (Joe and I were just tourists.) One such friend was Bill Spratling, the man who started the silver industry in Taxco and set up jewelry-making factories. In contrast to the big landowners and generals who acted as if the peons were slaves, he treated his employees fairly and well.

This was the period of the renaissance of the arts, most prominently David Alfaro Siqueiros, José Clemente Orozco, and Diego Rivera, whose historical murals in the atrium of the city hall of Cuernavaca are particularly wonderful. In Taxco, Joe also knew Hector Aguilar, a furniture maker, some of whose leather chairs are in our pool house today.

> Hearing in the late 1960s that Hector had settled on the Pacific coast in Zihuatanejo about 60 miles North of Acupulco, Joe and I donned bathing suits and walked up the beach for miles. Eventually, we found Hector and his wife and joined them for Cuba Libres ("Free Cubas" made of rum and Coca-Cola) and lunch.

Also in Taxco was Sherwood Anderson's widow, Elizabeth, an on-again, off-again friend of Faulkner's from his New Orleans days in the 1920s. Roark Bradford, who knew Faulkner and the Andersons in the same context, lived there too. Joe met Elizabeth and Roark in the early 1930s and introduced me to them later. Several of these expatriates visited us in Mississippi.

I went back with Pimmie in 1996. I will always love Mexico.

In the early 1930s, an American named Sterling Dickenson started the Instituto d'Allende, a school for art and the liberal arts. About 200 students came from outside the country, as well as many Mexicans. Joe and I took six-week courses in the winter. Joe took a fancy to one teacher who had never been to Spain and promptly bought him a plane ticket across the Atlantic.

We kept going to Mexico for about 15 years. Then, we discovered Europe. Why go to Mexico when you can go to Europe?

Yachting—The Golden Days

> We wanderers, ever seeking the lonelier way, begin no day where we have ended another day; and no sunrise finds us where sunset left us . . . Even while the earth sleeps, we travel.
> —*The Prophet*

> *We have gypsy blood in our veins on both sides—my mother traveled until she was 85, and Grandmother Frazier went to Mexico to visit Aunt Did and Uncle David Carter when she was past 70. The wanderlust came also from Mr. Will Dockery, who made frequent trips to Canada to fish and hunt. Had he lived today, he probably would have jetted around the world, just like us.*

We spent most of our vacations on the boat in Florida and the Caribbean—Key West, Fort Lauderdale, Nassau, and Cuba. Our first boat in a series, the Ruma, was a 65-foot power yacht. Joe piloted all our boats, but we always had professional help as well. Joe was a gracious captain and host.

Just before the war in 1939 for $12,000,[1] we bought the Azara, a three-masted schooner, from Ed Buckley of Houston (a cousin of Bill Buckley).

The Azara (1940).

At the helm.

Keith Somerville Dockery McLean

The Azara (a Greek character, which we never pronounced with a broad *A*), was "previously owned" not only by Ed but also by Canadian Commander Gooderham. The latter, after hosting the Duke of Windsor and the Queen of Spain on board, came in last in the Queen's Cup race between St. Petersburg, Florida, and San Sebastian, Spain, in the early 1920s.

At the waterline, the Azara was 110 feet long from the tip of the bowsprit to the stern; 125 feet including the full bowsprit (a piece of wood decorated with scroll work) protruding off the front. I like sailboats better than powerboats. We restored the interior, creating four double staterooms, so we could take three additional couples along. There was also a living and dining room. The crew was up forward in bunk beds for five. There were three heads (toilets), one for us, one for the guest quarters and one for the crew. The crew were south Alabama sailors who'd been in the business for generations. Joe had two of them on the payroll for 15 years.

We sailed her 16 years from 1940 to 1956 except during the war years, when we lent her to the maritime service for the war effort. Typically, we spent a couple of months a year on the Azara.

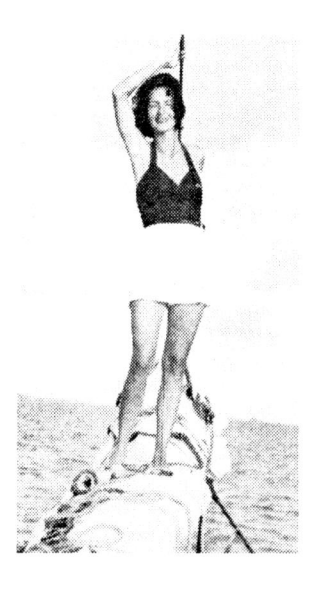

Pinup (photo by Sara Thesmar).

W<small>ANDERER FROM THE</small> D<small>ELTA</small>

We were aware that big things were happening but not quite what they would mean to use at home. We got our news by radio at 10 at night, and I remember H. V. Kaltenborn informing America of Hitler's invasion of Poland. Every night, Daddy dropped everything to go hear him.

> *There was no Public Radio then. I don't know how we survived.*

I had two miscarriages at four and six weeks before I had Douglas. I could conceive anytime, but had to take progestin to hold the fetus in.

After the third positive rabbit test, I went to bed for the biggest part of six weeks and took sedatives. Joe was so sweet.

All of my labors and deliveries were easy and were nearly natural childbirth—With all three, they had just started the saddle block when I delivered. The girls came two years apart.

> *It's amazing that anyone ever has the nerve to have a baby.*

Ashton married George Ingram III on February 25, 1940. The Ingrams had a long, happy marriage, and I feel particularly close to their children and grandchildren.

Aunt Lucy helped to end segregation in the American Association of University Women, on whose board she sat for many years.

Note

[1] About $148,000 in 2002 dollars.

1941–1945—THE WAR YEARS

Meanwhile, the war to end all wars hadn't.

On December 7, 1941, we heard the tragic news of the attack on Pearl Harbor, which marked the onset of World War II. It barely interrupted our happy life on the plantation, which was not truly to return to normal, however, for four years. We realized there was some anti-Semitism in Germany, but most of us—Mother excepted—didn't realize the extent of it.

No one we knew intimately died in the fighting, though many Mississippi men both black and white did. Dorothy Shands went to war in a Red Cross mobile unit in northern Africa, Sicily, and southern Italy. Her job, for which her merry approach to life well-suited her, was to entertain soldiers. In the course of her service, she broke her leg and was hospitalized in a navy hospital in Italy. Upon her return to Washington, D.C., she met and married John Martin before she landed, and immediately moved into a long-term job as a secretary to a Texas congressman.

Dorothy's mother resented her daughter's working rather than staying home with her children, but in fact the political wisdom and anecdotes from the Hill she brought back served their education well. Joe and I gave the Martins a big rehearsal dinner and reception at the time of their wedding.

Some friends became widows. Most remarried. For me at least, this war just stayed over across the ocean. When the world was collapsing in Europe in World War II, here I was having babies and meeting friends. Admittedly, we did roll some bandages for the Red Cross, which was much more helpful to our psyches than to the war effort. Bright spots were the births of our daughters during the years 1941–1944 just before and during the war years. I have written very little about my marvelous daughters in these pages to protect their privacy.

Mother was writing her "Dear Boys" letters and publishing them bimonthly in the *Bolivar Commercial* (January 15, 1943–August, 1945). In the introduction to the collection of these letters published in 1991, her editors wrote:

> Keith Frazier Somerville was a most remarkable individual. When reading her "Dear Boys" columns, one is continuously struck by the breadth and depth of coverage given to the many significant and wide-reaching topics she discussed. She perceptively described the important role played by women in the winning of the war. She offered substantial analytical comments about race relations, which were uncommon in wartime America, to say nothing of wartime Mississippi. She knew about and informed her readers of Nazi atrocities against Jews at a time when many people in much higher positions avoided the subject. She was proud of the multi-ethnic multi-faith composition of Bolivar County, and she hoped that the war would provide the opportunity for greater personal and social equality in Bolivar County, in Mississippi, in the United States, and throughout the world. Moreover, she enthusiastically embraced the ideals of the United Nations and was especially concerned that the Soviet Union and the United States remain friends and partners in the postwar era.[1]

Mother also wrote letters to black servicemen about the contributions they and their families were making to the war effort. She traveled to the nearby all-black town of Mound Bayou to talk to their families. She wrote eloquently about the importance of the cotton the town raised for the wartime effort, praised its citizens for buying more War Bonds than did people from Cleveland and Rosedale, and told the story of Annie Tutwiler, a black six-Gold-Star mother whose children were proving "to all the world that all races, creeds, and colors in America are in there fighting for . . . victory . . ."[2] I am particularly moved to remember her care to address the black troops' parents by last names, "Mrs._____" or "Mr._____," rather than—as was almost universal—calling black people by their first names or, worse: "Boy," "Uncle," "Gal," or "Auntie."

Her mother-in-law might have been dismayed by this egalitarianism but she might also have been proud of a column in which Mother proclaimed the value of "women who neither rivet nor weld, but remain behind to keep the home fires burning! We are to be called WINKS . . . Women in Numerous Kitchens."[3]

During those years, Ashton and the children, Ashton, II, and George, IV, lived in Mississippi for two or three years. (Elinor would come along a bit later.) Daddy was alive too at that point, and although they all spent a good deal of time out here with us at Dockery, they must have been pretty crowded both here and in Cleveland. I imagine Mother's cavalier approach to housekeeping must have bothered the Ingrams also. Both Ashton and I kept much cleaner houses than did Mother, who simply had different priorities.

We had it pretty easy down here during the War. This war, like the last one, was fought "over there" and did not touch me as it did others, though I was plenty lonely for my husband and anxious about the world situation, a lifelong obsession of mine. Joe was about 35, with a family of three and with a job in agriculture, and so was not drafted. He went to Washington in January of 1942 and volunteered to work in defense supplies, where he requisitioned—this is going to sound funny but is true—goose and duck feathers (among other things) to make down coats for our troops fighting in the winter in cold countries like Germany and France.

Lt. Dockery.

Joe was also sent to Mexico on a project Nelson Rockefeller headed. I am not quite sure what qualified him for this assignment. Perhaps his knowledge of business, Mexico, and the language. He came back home from time to time but was gone a lot from me and the children. Not satisfied with what he was doing for the war effort, he wanted to be in the armed forces and enlisted in the

Coast Guard, which stationed him in New Orleans, Mobile, and Grand Isle, Louisiana, and, towards the end of the war, on a large sailing schooner in the Gulf of Mexico making weather surveys. Later, when he returned to land duty, we stayed in New Orleans with him, renting a house in Metairie. Mother and Daddy were nearby, and I was able to leave the babies with them and join Joe wherever he was. While on patrol, he and his mates looked for submarines. They would have used police dogs to catch Germans coming ashore, but none ever came.

Several submarines were bombed off the coast and sunk, however.

We were much luckier than many of our friends who fought in terribly dangerous circumstances. Back home, we rolled bandages by hand, worked on blood drives, gave blood ourselves, worried over the casualties, and did without some gasoline, sugar, butter, and meat but, overall, suffered little.

The Allies defeated the Germans in June, 1945.

VJ Day

The official end of the war with Japan is etched into my memory. When we dropped the atomic bombs on Hiroshima and Nagasaki, the Japanese were finished. The peace treaty was signed on September 2, 1945, aboard the battleship Missouri in the Pacific. We were in Tennessee, when we heard the news broadcast over the car radio at about 6 o'clock in the evening. I was so excited that I hurried off to celebrate, leaving the ignition on and killing the battery.

Mother and I and the children were at Monteagle, in a large rented two-story house next to Grandmother Somerville's home. Ashton was there too with little Ashton and baby George. Big George had been working for the Tennessee Valley Authority. He volunteered for the Navy during the last six months of war and was in England when peace came. Joe was in New York being mustered out of the service.

After the broadcast, almost everyone on the mountain rushed down to the mall in the center of the assembly grounds. Each of us pulled the cord and rang the big bell, which is now housed in its own bell tower. It rings at set times—twilight, 11 AM, and so on—and in commemoration of important events.

We held the babies up to let them pull too. This was Mother's idea: She wanted them to remember that historic night. Later, we put the children to bed and stayed up until 3 AM listening to broadcasts.

Death also touched us personally that day. Joe called me from New York with the tragic news that Oscar Levingston of Ruleville, Joe's closest friend and the man who had handled Dockery during the war, had been killed that night in an auto wreck. His was a tremendous loss for us, for the community, and, most of all of course, for his widow. A friend from Monteagle drove me to Nashville, where I took the overnight train to Memphis. There Daddy met me, and we attended the funeral together.

In April of 1945, our nation had been shocked to learn, also by radio, that our President, Franklin Roosevelt, had died suddenly in Warm Springs. It was a stunning loss, as he had been a strong and charismatic leader in time of crisis. He had both passionate partisans and detractors. Mother loved him and arranged a tribute of red, white, and blue flowers on her dining room table. I had a lot of admiration for him as a leader. I am a lifelong Democrat, of course, part of the solid Democratic South, but Eleanor Roosevelt was a pariah here because of her racial positions. I thought she was marvelous, however, and Joe and Lucy Howorth knew both Roosevelts in Washington and liked them. Daddy was not real strong for Roosevelt. I don't recall either antipathy or positive feelings toward FDR in Joe, but he probably shared his region's dislike of the first lady. Joe was not very interested in politics—certainly not as interested as I.

The girls got a good primary education in a demonstration school at Delta State. It was exclusive, with about 30 children in each grade, kindergarten through sixth grade, and it gave them a good start. After learning to read properly at that school, the three went on to public schools in Cleveland, which were still pretty good academically.

I was a typical midcentury mother of growing children. The car pools were constant—back and forth, back and forth, to play practices, music lessons, dancing classes, visits to friends. There was also volunteer work. For example, I chaired the PTA planning program.

The three girls and me in front of Dockery's fireplace, 1947.

Daddy died of a heart attack in 1946 at a bar association in meeting in Jackson 17 years after the car accident. He was only 59, though I, at 31, thought he was really very old. He was active throughout his life, and his was a good way to go, doing something he loved. Joe and I were in New York at the Waldorf. When we arrived home the following day, Ashton was already there.

Mother would be a widow for the next 31 years.

Our Glory Days

The years after the war were happy ones for America. Industry was being converted from military to peacetime uses, and times were prosperous.

Joe and a friend.

In the late 1940s, the Duke and Duchess of Windsor and Mrs. Truman came to Mardi Gras in New Orleans. Wallis Simpson, beautiful in lavender and amethysts, made a deep, gracious bow to the carnival queen. Bess Truman was gauche, merely nodding briefly to the Mardi Gras royalty. I wore a pale-coral satin floor-length ball gown purchased on Park Avenue in New York City.

At the Delta Council in Cleveland, William Faulkner made a speech, saying much the same things as he did in his Nobel address, "Man will not merely endure, he will prevail."

Notes

[1] *Dear Boys: World War II Letters from a Woman Back Home* (Judy Barrett Litoff and David C. Smith, Eds.) (Jackson: University Press of Mississippi, 1991), p. 15.

[2] P. 9.

[3] P. 155.

BACK ON THE WATERS

The war over, we got the Azara back and continued our sybaritic vacations.

Though the girls came with us sometimes, they mostly stayed in Cleveland with Etta Johnson, a woman of German extraction with big bosoms and a big heart who had been a family employee of the Dockerys since Joe Rice was a baby. It was unusual to have a white nanny in this area.

Miss Etta had been Joe's nanny, and now she was his daughters'. She stayed with us for several years and had a profound influence on our children. She may have been too lenient at times, but how the girls loved her. They also stayed with our childless friends the Bedwells and with Mother.

When we could, we took the girls along on the yacht. We had them on the Azara when they were as young as three, five, and seven. Baby Keith dove off the bowsprit of the boat when she was three. (We taught the girls to swim at about age three.) The girls occasionally flew to meet us. Once, when Keith was 10 and Kay 12, they had to spend the night in the Miami airport alone en route to join us in Nassau.

Mother also went along with friends in the early 1950s; once, Ashton and George joined us in Florida with their children. We all swam at Destin, sailed in and out of the Gulf of Mexico, and, in general, had a lovely, luxurious time.

From Gulfport, Mississippi, it took three to four days to Key West and from there, it was "only 90 miles" to Cuba, then the "Paris of the Caribbean," about a day's sail. Our trips to Cuba began right after we were married. We made many friends—among them, Merrill Matsinger of Merrill Lynch and Commodore Pozo—at the Havana yacht club. We'd go to see fishing friends in Texas or New Orleans and then sail to Cuba. We went ashore at a place called Veradero Beach three hours' drive from Havana, where we met Winthrop and Vivian Smith. Winthrop joined Merrill Lynch shortly thereafter. We made many connections—the world seemed smaller then. Everyone seemed to know everyone else—at least most people of a certain class recognized their peers.

We also began to find friends among artists, writers, and musicians, and we began to collect art. We started out by buying prints and other copies and then graduated to discovering original contemporary art and artists, including that of Edna Taçon, Karl Larsson, Adelle Lemm, and Edna Hibel; my cousin Jim Fort; and Mississippians Bill Dunlap (who now anchors a Washington TV art show), Malcolm Norwood, Martha Virden, Bill Lester, Emma Lytle, Joe Howorth, Pam Mathews, and Nan Sanders.

In the late 1960s, we bought Edna Taçon's painting of a pregnant girl and Christian symbols on the installment plan.

When Joe wanted to play, he did with a flair. For example, in Acapulco, we hired a plane and flew about 40 miles along the coast to spend the day swimming and walking at a particularly lovely beach, having a special lunch, seeing people. We'd walk down to a beach and slide into our bathing suits crouched behind bushes or palm trees.

Before lunch, we'd often drink Cuba libres.

There was no fear about skin cancer then, and we doused ourselves in pure "cocobutter" (coconut oil) and sunbathed. Beautiful and brown, we looked good.

KEITH SOMERVILLE DOCKERY MCLEAN

Joe and I saunter on the beach in the 1950s.

We were part of the high life in Cuba. Joe liked gambling, and he didn't lose much. He shot craps and played the stock market. We played bridge, poker, and gin; we read and swam. We visited the casino; we entertained friends on board; we sailed our little Sunfish, and we water-skied (well, some of us did). There was a darling spinet on the Azara, and we had lots of sing-alongs. Our favorite? "There'll Always Be an England," along with Cole Porter's "Love for Sale" and "Night and Day," and anything by the Gershwins.

We also enjoyed Nassau before it became overcrowded and when it seemed truly British. There has seldom been a place more English than the British Colonial Hotel overlooking Nassau Harbor.

Joe played lots of tennis with Lloyd Budge, who later came to visit us at Dockery, and who frequently complimented Joe on his strong backhand. Lloyd autographed his book to Joe "You're the only player—aside from Brother Don—who plays with me in the right court." Joe persuaded Lloyd to coach at Joe's "alma mater," Mississippi State.

We did give some marvelous and exciting house parties for the girls and their friends during school holidays, usually on the Gulf Coast around Destin where the turquoise-blue waters are unsurpassed. Our daughters' friends from those years, now in their 50s and 60s, still tell me of their happy memories of those trips.

Shortly after *The Power of Positive Thinking* was published in 1952, Joe and I went to Norman Vincent Peale's Marble Collegiate Church in New York, walking together from 24th Street up to 80th. Later we met the impressive Dr. Peale at the Metropolitan Club.

In New York, Joe and I twice saw Gershwin's *Porgy and Bess*, an in-depth treatment of black mores in the South, an eye-opener and one of my lifelong favorites.

In the Delta, Saralie and I gave a two-piano recital at the Cleveland Women's Club for an audience of about 70. We played Delibes's *Dolly Suite* and a Jamaican rhumba.

Piano duet, 1950.

European Sojourns

In early 1952, Joe and I made the first of perhaps 24 practically annual trips to the Continent. We often went by ship, staying for about a month and a half during January and February, which were not farming months.

I'm off—Our first transatlantic ocean voyage.

Now I can't stand to stay away from Dockery that long.

Although we also sometimes flew, the ocean crossings were particularly wonderful sources of many friendships. Whether by ship or plane, I will never fail to be thrilled and moved at the sight of the Statue of Liberty in New York harbor.

We often traveled on Italian lines, including the Vulcania, the Saturnia, and (Joe alone) on the ill-fated Andrea Doria, fortunately not on the voyage when she became an Italian restaurant for sharks.

Our first trip was a grand tour—Paris, Spain, and Italy. Our Air France constellation flight arrived in Paris four hours early thanks to strong westerly winds. The three-and-a-half-hour flight was extraordinarily fast in the 1950s (and even for today), when flying to Europe was the new way to go but generally took hours and required refueling, often in Ireland or Iceland. We checked in at the Plaza Athenée and spent most of that day being driven around the most beautiful of cities in a light misty rain which shrouded Notre Dame and gave the beautiful Alexander III bridge an added glamour.

On the Vulcania.

Next day we flew to Spain, planning to return to Paris at the end of the trip and arriving in Madrid in the late afternoon, descending through a spectacular sunset streaked with those very Spanish colors of orange, red, and bright pink. We stayed at the Ritz, then and now one of the world's greatest and most luxurious hotels. We fell in love with both the country and the rug in our hotel room and, for about $350 (now about $2,500), had it copied for our dining room floor at Dockery.

It remains there still, only a bit the worse for wear.

We rented a car and took a day trip to El Escorial and visited both

Philip II's 16th-century tomb, and the high altar where he passed the time during retirement winding his dozens of clocks.

Then on to Italy: Rome, down the Amalfi coast (particularly its prettiest city, Ravello), and the Italian Riviera. Joe and I always kept moving, usually staying in one place only for a couple of days. With rare exceptions, we stayed in hotels, but in Florence, we spent about a week living with an aristocratic Italian family down on its luck, high above the city near the reproduction of David in the Piazziale Michelangelo. On that occasion, I remember lunching in Fiesole and hearing a summer piano concert in the Boboli Gardens after walking past the wonderful statue of the little fat man sitting on a marble turtle at the garden's entrance. He is even funnier than the Buddhas.

Sometimes we had guides and chauffeur-driven cars; once, we bought a Mercedes-Benz in Stuttgart, drove it around Germany, France, and Portugal, and shipped it home.

The Mercedes at Cabo San Luca, Portugal, the westernmost point of Europe.

The Prado introduced us to Goya, Velasquez, Rivera, El Greco, and Murillo, and intensified my lifelong love, discovered with the Howorths in Washington and the Evanses in New York, of visiting galleries and museums. My favorite art movement at first was Impressionism; now it's Abstract Expressionism. My taste, however, is "catholic." I love European landscapes, Bill Dunlap's "Cattle Tracks" (a 1970 landscape of the Shenandoah Valley which hangs at Dockery), and my cousin Jim Fort's abstract wooden sculptures.

> *There were no museums in Cleveland when I was 38. Now there are!*

In southern Spain, we met Joe's glamorous friend "Tony" from Texas, who had married Rafael Osborne, a sherry baron.

> *"Tony" from San Antonio; "Hondo" from Hondo; "Slim" from... The South?*

My admiration for Tony's designer clothes led us to a Balenciaga showing, where I bought, for about $75 (now $500), an avant-garde black wool suit.

> *I still bring it and certain other Balenciaga pieces out for extraordinary occasions like costume balls or special dinner parties.*

The linens for Tony's beds were embroidered by nuns, and it was said that she took her own special bedding along when she traveled.

Tony's first husband, whom she divorced, was a Mexican bullfighter, and she still had friends among the elite bull fighters. When Joe visited the Osbornes later at their vineyard at Jerez de la Frontera, he swore that Tony's bodyguard, another bullfighter, slept at the door of her bedroom.

- On our next trip to Spain, we met Nuria and Salvador Marsal on the Talgo, the fast train from Madrid to Barcelona, and stopped with them in Barcelona. We exchanged visits frequently with them from then on, and the Marsals gave us several of Nuria's father's works, including a wonderful oil, several etchings, and a large book.

> *The Duranchamps Museum in Barcelona now features his work.*

- We made numerous return visits to the lovely Iberian Peninsula including Portugal. We played lots of bridge. No matter whom I played with, I won. (Just luck.)

- Our Viennese visits to the Ingrams in the 1950s were great fun. They were wonderful hosts, and George was like the brother I never had. I especially remember Ashton's expert ways with flowers and food. We also met the Ingrams in Italy, spending a memorable long weekend in Portofino, enjoying ourselves together in Santa Margarita, and going to France as a foursome. Still, our interaction as couples seemed somehow superficial.

  > *I've always been sad that something—I've never known exactly what—went wrong between us sisters. When Ashton and I were together, she complained angrily that I tended to "overanalyze."*

- In the summer of 1958, after my recovery from a third miscarriage (sad, but I was in my mid-40s, a better time to be thinking about becoming a grandmother than a mother), Joe took me to San Sebastian on the Bay of Biscayne (north coast of Spain), where we spent a week at the most stylish resort hotel of the area. We went to the beach daily, and I got well quickly. It was there that we made friends with Judi Dench, the marvelous English actress, and her parents.

> *Later, long after we lost touch with her, she was made a Dame. What a pleasure to watch her brilliant career! She was especially wonderful, I think, as Elizabeth, I, in* Shakespeare in Love. *The critics agreed, awarding her an Oscar for best supporting actress although she was on screen for only minutes.*

From Spain, we flew to Brussels to visit their wonderful World's Fair. I think that must have been the first time I was really aware of the Muslim world. The Persians and Saudis had wonderful pavilions. Also new to me were the beautiful crafts of Thailand. The Soviet pavilion, however, was fundamentally boring: Lots of huge grey machines but also many books.

- We took the girls along on the grand tour of Europe in 1960. Keith was finishing high school, and Kay and Douglas were in college. Joe and I and the older girls flew to Paris and met Keith and her Lausanne classmates in Rome and again in Vienna, where we visited with Ashton and the Ingrams. There, we heard *La Boheme,* sung in German!
  Then, it was on to ancient ruins in Rome, in Florence to the Academia (Kay was taken with Michelangelo's David), and to Switzerland. We drove in rented cars and hired guides. Finally, our daughters accompanied us home on the Île de France.

- Covent Garden, 1972, with the Metropolitan Opera Guild

- On the Italian Riviera, on a narrow ribbon of road cut shallowly into the side of towering seaside precipices, a car suddenly sped towards our rental car. There was nowhere for Joe to go except into the wall. He was flung against the gearshift and was laid up in France for four days. His knee never fully recovered.

- Hite and I and Kay returned to Barcelona in 1989. Granddaughter Louise Derbes, spending her junior year of high school there, connected with a friend of a friend of the Marsals as well.

WAY BACK DOWN IN DIXIE

Things—race relations—began to change in the '50s when I was in my 40s.

> "What's to be gained by talking about it?" [Elizabeth Spencer was asked in Carrollton, Mississippi, in the 1950s].
> "Well, everything is to be lost by *not* talking about it," [she] could have replied.
> —*Landscapes of the Heart* (1998, p. 313)

Carrollton is about 50 miles from Cleveland. In contrast to what my friend Elizabeth reports there, Mother and I had long and memorable conversations about the unfairness of the lives blacks led compared to those of whites . . . What's going to happen is going to happen, we agreed.

Each of our daughters transferred at age 14 to the Lausanne School for Girls in Memphis (a small boarding school where a favorite cousin, Walter Coppedge, was headmaster). They graduated in 1958, 1960, and 1962, respectively. I hated to have them away from us, and if I had my life to live over, I would have moved and lived across the street from the school in Memphis while they were there. As it was, I was always running back and forth to Memphis to bring them things and be with them. They didn't like being away at first, but they got used to it, and, otherwise, they would have had to go seven miles away to the terrible school in Ruleville, which offered no science, only two years of math, and no Latin or any other foreign language. The Ruleville school wouldn't have prepared them for college. (We were gerrymandered into the Sunflower County schools.)

> Yes, the Ruleville school also became mostly black.
> The main place where integration hit us was in education.
> Compared to Douglas, Kay, and Keith's schools in Cleveland, the level of learning curve was much lower in the Ruleville school. One's bridge and tennis games improve when one competes with good players. The same goes for education. From the standpoint of college preparation, we didn't want our daughters in the Ruleville school, not because of the integration issue.
> I can't speak for Joe.
> I always found integration was worth trying. It's easy to theorize now; however, I admit frequently that I am an armchair liberal. The girls' move to Lausanne in Memphis was part of the "white flight" into private schools.

Our daughters complain that, even in the 1950s, they were not reared to have careers, but to get married and have children. Like my father, Joe felt his daughters should have some kind of fall-back profession, so that they wouldn't be totally dependent on a man. I agreed.

Life went on as usual at Dockery, except that Joe planted rice and soybeans as well as cotton. Joe's rice crops made him a pioneer in the early 1950s. Rice harvest comes in September; cotton and soybeans in October or November.

We lost a few of our treasures when the commissary burned on a hot August afternoon in about 1953, probably due to a fire resulting from spontaneous combustion (or old wiring or rats). It had been closed since after the war, when the office moved down to the highway.

The Dockery commissary (photo by Cullen Bedwell).

We didn't suffer great damage, though I miss our old London-style telephone booth with ring central—the operator would answer when you picked up the receiver and you'd ask her to ring so-and-so. (If you asked for someone whom she knew—and she knew just about everyone—she'd let you know if your party was unavailable. For example, "Sorry, Mary Brown is not home. She will be out until four playing bridge at the Smith plantation in Greenville.") That was the only telephone there when Joe and I were married, something I found dangerous. If there were an emergency, the phone was a block away. So he had one installed at the house.

The commissary had long been a gathering place and company store. It was probably built around 1900. The brick may have been homemade at Dockery.

Steve Derbes took some of it to make a patio in his and Keith's New Orleans garden. I am so pleased.

We lost mostly old papers, records, and furniture, but also bits of history—photos going all the way back to when Will Dockery settled here in 1895. We've left the picturesque ruins.

In 1954, Judge Lucy retired as general counsel of the War Claims Commission and returned to Mississippi. She and Joe Howorth, an artist as well as a lawyer, made Cleveland a livelier place.

Ole Miss Law School (painting by Joe Howorth).

That same year, the first White Citizen's Council was held in nearby Indianola (27 miles away), a horrible organization destined to cause great harm. Other groups soon joined it, and within three months a state association of councils was formed in Winona. By 1956, the White Citizens' Council of America, with members nationwide, opened its headquarters in Jackson, where it received state funding.

Changing Times

In 1955, Rosa Parks stayed in her seat on the bus in Montgomery, Alabama.

The same year, Emmet Till, a 14-year-old boy from Chicago, was mutilated and murdered after he whistled at a white woman (and perhaps asked her for a date) in Money, Mississippi, under 40 miles from Cleveland.

> *I just finished reading* Wolf Whistle, *by Delta native Lewis Norden. It's a tragic story based on the murder of Emmet Till.*
>
> *Horrible. I speculate that a lot of people* tried *to do something, but they backed down in the face of the many dangerous people on the other side.*
>
> *We all* talked *of nothing else.*

Douglas was a camp leader at Deerwood, a wonderful horseback-riding and swimming camp, in North Carolina. She went two months each summer, starting at about 14 for three years. Every two years, one of her sisters followed her. While they played, Joe and I farmed, visited them, and spent time on the yacht.

During the 1950s, my work on behalf of the arts really took off.

> *There was not as much dissemination of information about the arts in Mississippi 50 years ago as there is today, and there was no consensus about the value even of people now recognized as giants, like William Faulkner. The* Faulkner and Yoknapatowpha Conferences *(annually) didn't get underway until 1974, 12 years after his death.*

Upon its creation in 1956, I was appointed to the Mississippi Arts Commission Board, which gave me its Governor's Award for volunteerism in 1995. I continued on the Board until my second term expired in 1964, and I became too busy to serve further.

As a member of the building committee of Calvary Episcopal

Church, I began in 1956 to help interview the architects who would build the new church, where we'd worship from then until the 21st century. The beautiful old church became our parish house.

End of an Era

In the 1950s, life continued on the Azara much as it had before the War.

Anchored in the Bahamas or off Destin in Florida, we'd dive off the boat and swim and come up and breakfast on deck. Our one-eyed chef fixed food stocked up in the deep freeze. The rest of the day, we'd spend swimming, fishing, sunbathing, reading books, and listening to the radio. We played a lot of bridge. In the afternoons, we'd take the small sailboat out or go into the markets. There was also waterskiing, several little motorboats, and a speedboat on stanchions—15-foot steel arms that swung out—like cranes for lifeboats, as well as a Sunfish for one or two persons. Joe taught me how to solo, and we taught the children. We all went way out, across Destin bay.

The British West Indies people have a delightful accent.

In Nassau, we'd lunch at a hotel. At night, we'd have drinks on board before dinner. Lots of "Cuba Libres." Americans were not much into wine in those days—that came later. We drank gin and tonic and planter's punches in 10-ounce glasses. The punch was made of rum and pineapple and orange juice served with a cherry. Rum is one of strongest drinks there is—it can really be dangerous. Nonetheless, we brought back a lot of good but inexpensive rum.

Joe got rid of the Azara in 1956 for a number of reasons. By the 1950s, it was difficult to find suitable and competent crews of four able-bodied men to sail her.

Also, as time went by, guests were not always as available to join us in those yachting parties. Many older people were not as enthusiastic about adventurous trips as our younger friends had been, and Joe wanted the girls to travel widely, unlimited by the vagaries of the sea and the winds and the Azara. In addition, although he didn't burden me with the knowledge at the time, being skipper of the Azara demanded constant watchful attention.

Eventually, unable to find a buyer and wanting to shed the responsibility, Joe donated the Azara as a tax write-off. It went to the Lightning and Transients Corporation for a Geophysical Year survey of weather conditions in the Great Lakes. While the corporation did significant work for several years, disaster struck when the Azara was hauled out onto inadequate drydock and fell off the supports, cracking its marvelous, unique bronze hull.

She had to be scrapped.

What a tragedy that there may never again be such a vessel.

> *It turns out, however, that the days of bronze hulls were numbered anyway because they poison the water.*

And Back at the Ranch

We continued to leave the girls with Miss Etta, until we didn't need her anymore. Then, we retired her, and she went to Memphis. Knowing Joe, he probably gave a comfortable pension.

> *It's sad that in our society there's no dignified and important role for servants.*

The girls also stayed with their grandmother, who was wild about them and took them to dancing school, read to them, and played cards—solitaire, double solitaire, and canasta—with them.

Ashton and I had skipped our debuts during the Depression, but times were considerably better financially at Dockery in the 1960s than in Cleveland in the 1930s, and the Dockery daughters came out in Greenville and Memphis both. Walker Percy was at a debut ball in Greenville I also attended, because his daughter was being presented. He sat behind me, and I began to correspond with him at about that time, to congratulate him on the books.

> *I wish I had called on him before he died in 1990.*

The Rosalie girls in Natchez.

Family portrait—the Dockerys.

Keith Somerville Dockery McLean

Tumult and Celebration

Joe emceed a debut ball in Greenville. The young women came out to the triumphal march from *Aida,* which always reminds me of Leontyne Price (born in Laurel, Mississippi, about 200 miles from Cleveland, when I was 13). Hers is the most beautiful voice I have ever heard.

> *I knew the Chisholms, people who realized that incredible talents transcend races, who sent Leontyne Price to Wilberforce. I heard her in concert several times in Mississippi. She received the lifetime achievement award from the Mississippi Institute of Arts and Letters in 2000, an award her brother accepted in her name. My friends the Chisholms, who had employed Leontyne's mother as a helper, funded much of Leontyne's education. The families stayed close, and Leontyne Price went to Jean Chisholm's funeral in New York City in 1999.*

Leontyne Price

Born in 1927 to a carpenter and a midwife and domestic servant with a lovely soprano voice, Leontyne Price received excellent voice and piano training from early girlhood. Thanks both to her own talent and perseverance and to the Chisholm's generosity, she continued her education at the College of Educational and Industrial Arts in Wilberforce, Ohio. She next went to Juilliard School of Music on a full tuition scholarship. Her astonishing talent led her to New York appearances and a European tour. In 1952, she took the powerful role of Bess in a revival of Gershwin's *Porgy and Bess.* The next two decades were studded with triumphant performances in the world's great opera houses and recital halls in New York, London, Milan, Vienna, and San Francisco, as well as on television. Throughout the 1950s, Price broadened her career as an opera singer by starring in a number of works in packed recital halls and opera stages and on tele-

> vision. In 1964, she was awarded the Presidential Freedom Award, and the following year, she won the Italian Award of Merit.
>
> I heard her in *Il Trovatore* about 1975.

I was among the founders of Amici, an opera appreciation group that directs and helps fund Metropolitan Opera auditions. Between 1970 and 1995, these took place at Ole Miss.

In 1995, with advice and help from other board members, we moved the auditions to the wonderful Bologna Performing Arts Center at Delta State. Off and on since 1970, I have served as Amici's president.

I also served on the board of the Metropolitan Opera National Council, which meets annually in Manhattan and, on occasion, regionally in places as distant as Texas and New Orleans.

Both of these are volunteer positions.

In the spring of 1961, part of Dockery, including our front yard, was underwater thanks to an enormous flood of the Sunflower River.

In 1961, Kay married Tom Clark in a gala Christmas wedding at Calvary Episcopal Church in Cleveland.

The same year, Joe was King of the Cotton Carnival in Memphis, a high honor. There were parades and parties. He made many speeches promoting cotton. Because cities named Memphis sit on both the Mississippi and the Nile, people gave their clubs names like "Osiris."

Our first grandchild, Carolyn Clark, was born. So were 13 basset pups.

1963—John F. Kennedy Assassinated

Such a shocking tragedy for our country to lose our elegant young president. I was at a Pi Beta Phi luncheon the day that he died.

And Civil Rights

I am politically oriented—I always have been. I think that it's a cardinal sin not to vote; however, in the early 1960s in the Deep South, as far as a black person coming to dinner at a white's house ... It just did not happen. A sandwich or a bowl of soup in the kitchen instead. While narrowing, the splits between blacks and whites are still prevalent today, even between us and the black people we know and love.

Like most Southern towns, Cleveland has had black and white sections since its origin. We have upper- and lower-crust versions of both—fancy big houses with manicured lawns and driveways and slums with dirt yards often full of drifting trash. If you don't have grass or a lawn mower, what's the alternative?

> *I see a great deal of hope now that race relations will continue to improve, particularly thanks to wider educational opportunities. Delta State is helping this cause wonderfully. Soon—within 25 to 40 years or less—both the blacks and we will be a minority. Now, however, a black and white couple is still unusual in Mississippi, and I expect elsewhere. It's hard for administrators at Delta State to find qualified black professors who want to come and live here.*

In the 1960s, there were great big billboard signs on Mississippi highways and byways saying that Martin Luther King was a Communist. Medgar Evers was gunned down in his driveway 150 miles from Cleveland in 1963, and the next year voting rights workers Andrew Goodman, James Earl Chaney, and Michael Henry Schwerner were murdered somewhere between Philadelphia (143 miles) and Meridian (238 miles).

There were marches in Selma. The younger people in my daughters' generation (in their 20s in the 1960s) were more receptive to the Civil Rights movement than older people who advanced more slowly. The assassinations of 1968 shocked us horribly. Martin Luther King had been in Marks, Mississippi—only 50 miles from Cleveland—the day he was murdered.

I had just driven home from Memphis, where I had been obliviously visiting friends on the day he was killed there. When I arrived at Dockery, Joe told me what had happened. As we reeled from Dr. King's assassination, Bobby Kennedy was murdered. Sermons in churches—black and white alike—deplored the killings.

> *What we've done and what we've left undone comes out pretty strong. It's embarrassing. Life just went on. And I recognize to my sorrow that Molière was right:* "It is not what we do, but also what we do not do, for which we are accountable."

We would hear that something "bad" had happened somewhere but never much more than that.

Southern Christian churches, black and white alike, were often proactive in the Civil Rights movement. The Episcopal church opened its doors and invited anyone to come in when that kind of invitation simply was "not done." Some of the United Methodists encouraged black women to participate, particularly in Greenville. Baptist Will D. Campbell's memoir, *Brother to a Dragonfly*, describes his conversion to the Civil Rights movement. In 1962, James Meredith matriculated at Ole Miss, while Episcopal Bishop Duncan Gray II heroically tried to quiet mobs moiling on the front steps of the campus under a Confederate flag. Campbell also wrote Gray's biography, taking its title, *And Also with You*, from *The Book of Common Prayer*.

> *Mississippi Bishop Duncan Gray, I (1898–1996) had the first parish in Cleveland in the 1920s (his wife was a McCrady of Oxford). His son, Mississippi Bishop Duncan Gray II (1926–) was rector of St. Peter's and the hero of Ole Miss in the 1960s. His son, Mississippi Bishop Duncan Gray III (1949–) helped and comforted us as Joe lay dying. His son, Duncan Gray IV (1980–) is 20.*
>
> *Our friendship with the Gray family goes back three generations and blesses us all.*

During the riots, Hite took his daughter Kim home from the Oxford campus, returning her there in a couple of days, when he felt she would again be safe there.

Our daughter Keith lived with an activist couple in Memphis, the Goodmans. He was Jewish and his wife and children were Episcopalian. A lot of people, including Mary Goodman, marched with the Memphis garbage collectors the day before Martin Luther King was killed there.

A woman in nearby Ruleville, Fannie Lou Hamer, was a black leader almost like Rosa Parks. So many of these black leaders were women. There's an area in Ruleville dedicated to Mrs. Hamer. She spoke out and led black people to assert their rights as voters.

> *Mrs. Hamer, whose family sharecropped on other people's land, had a fourth-grade education and was a victim of forced sterilization.[1] Still, she was the first in her area to stand up and register. Her family was evicted from their land. At one point, a mob of men beat her nearly to death.*
>
> *In 1968, she led the challenge to the national Democratic party in Chicago.*
>
> *"Wake up America!"*
>
> *"This little light of mine . . .* [a spiritual made famous by Leontyne Price].
>
> *On feminism:*
>
> *"Baby, I don't know if I could spell it, but I know what it's about."*

About Civil Rights and integration, Joe was a pragmatist who marched with most of his peers, including Daddy but not Mother. I went along with the prevailing power structure, and I'm not proud of that now. If I had not been married to Joe, I might have been out on the streets marching with the protestors. But I was, and I didn't.

Helpers

Virdie Mullins Hugger came to work for me in 1962 and stayed 20 years, quickly becoming my lifelong friend as well as helper. Her grandfather, Tab Block, had worked for Daddy. The whole family were activists except for Virdie, who said, "leave everything alone."

From Resignation Came Activism

One of Virdie's cousins was Sam Block, a Civil Rights leader active in the Student Nonviolent Coordinating Committee (SNCC) around Cleveland in the 1960s when he was in his 50s. He died in 2000 in Los Angeles. I was invited to his funeral, which friends said was an impressive and moving gathering. Lizzie, who worked for Aunt Eleanor Shands, was his grandmother. His sister, Margaret Block, is writing a book about her brother.

When she learned that Mother was into genealogies, Virdie asked Mother to "make me a family tree." Her mother was an Indian, so the tree was red and black and white. "Put us all in it," she asked Mother.

> *After Joe died, Virdie's husband got sick, and she had to retire and care for him. Still, she used to come to Dockery on special occasions to help—She's a fabulous cook.*
>
> *We did not pay benefits or vacations to our workers. No one did. We did, however, pay some of them—including Virdie—pensions.*
>
> *Virdie came to see me recently at about 89. She has had a stroke, and, like me with this broken wrist in 2000, hates not to be able to do for herself. We're both in better shape now, two years later.*

The Blues

We didn't even know about the Blues until late in the 1960s, though Joe was more aware of the music being made at Dockery than was I. A man who called from Tulane doing research told us that some recordings made on our plantation go back to the late '20s and that Charlie Patton had been singing on nearby porches Saturday nights for decades. In 1941, Joe also talked to Alan Lomax, whose Library of Congress folk recordings are legendary.[2]

> *A black man on Dockery, Ruffian Scott, is the oldest person today who remembers anything about the blues. In his low 90s, he's in terrible health. His divorced former wife came back from Chicago to care for him and nursed him until she died. In 1999, a Delta State researcher interviewed the Scotts and forgot to tell me that they had been unable to pay their water bill and their water had been cut off. When I did find out, I tried to help them get it turned back on.*
>
> *After his wife died, Ruffian moved to his daughter's, in Utica, for caretaking.*

Joy and Sadness

In 1967, Keith married Steve Derbes on a happy, hot August day. Two years later, Douglas married Bill Porteous high on Dockery Hill.

> *My sister, Ashton, had gone through a serious psychiatric trauma after her family's return from Vienna. She was depressed, even suicidal. To help her, Mother and I went up to Washington to be interviewed in case what we revealed could help Ashton. The doctors never could understand the cause, however, and neither could she nor George. They came up with the finding that her depression originated when she found she couldn't stand hot climates—she did have to be*

evacuated from their State Department post in Baghdad, for example, but I don't recall her complaining more about Mississippi heat than anyone else. Then, to some extent, she turned against things in Mississippi, although she would come down just to be with Mother and, to a lesser extent, me.

Notes

[1] Freedom of choice means freedom to have children as well as not to have them.

[2] In 1941 and 1942, the folklorist Alan Lomax, now in his 80s, visited the Mississippi Delta to document the region's African-American folk music. One of his major objectives was to record the Delta's most famous cultural product: the blues. "Mississippi, the Blues Lineage" (Rounder 11661-1825), whose contents Lomax selected before a stroke incapacitated him in the 1990s, represents his early-'40s Delta blues fieldwork.

The work of Lomax and his father exposed socio-cultural situations in the South, putting the blues into "a frame of reference that validated black experience, and challenged the institutionalized racism of the nation."

—Quotation from the Internet, no author given "The Sound of Music," *Southern Journey: The Alan Lomax Collection Vol. I-VI*

TIMOR MORTIS

I spent a lot of time in hospitals during the 1970s. We learned at last of my gluten intolerance, technical name—*nontropical spru*. I may have had it all my life but was only actively sick for three months. I had serious diarrhea, couldn't keep anything down, and lost 20 pounds, which I could ill-afford to do without.

On a gluten-free diet, I was well shortly.

Ashton and Mother and me (1967).

Here I am, wearing Joe's mother's dress at a benefit party at Dockery for Cleveland's Crosstie Arts Council. Aunt Lucy, Joe Howorth, and Joe Rice are in the background. Costumes were supposed to be from 1908.

Dr. Ted Lathram, a psychiatrist in Memphis, treated Joe for 6 to 10 sessions starting in about 1975. Joe, understandably, became depressed after he had stomach and colon cancer. Although the doctors surgically "cured" him, he had to have a colostomy.

We had a wonderful marriage, even during the last six or eight years as Joe grew sicker. When he became ill, he became more dependent on me. For example, I did most of the driving. We would sit by the fire, and I'd read to him. Those were sweet, memorable times.

Suddenly, within a few weeks, Joe became seriously

disoriented, and it was discovered that he was suffering from a brain tumor. We had the best medical care imaginable while Joe was in the Baptist Hospital in Memphis, but three weeks after surgery, Joe developed pneumonia.

I asked the doctor, "Can Joe ever get better?"

"No."

"Then why treat the pneumonia?"

Our friend Duncan Gray III, then on his way to becoming a bishop, was attentive and helpful to the family. Duncan administered the last rites, Joe's breathing eased, and he went to sleep. I was with Joe when he died on July 2, 1982. When I remember him, I think of birds, the sky, and the sea—not of his decline into illness and death.

His body was cremated—I think of fire and the rays of sun consuming his corpse—and his ashes were scattered among the jonquils on our hill in accordance with his wishes.

I want my ashes scattered at Dockery as well.

His funeral on July 4 brought many, many friends to Dockery. Duncan conducted a family communion service, and a memorial service took place at the Baptist church on Dockery grounds. It was beautiful, moving, appropriate . . . and left me shattered.

Eulogies

After Joe's death, Douglas said, "Daddy just tried to take us everywhere." He wanted the girls to have good educations, and he considered travel to be part of education.

Joe took *me* on a long, wonderful journey of 44 years. Losing him was like having a limb amputated. I will always be grateful to Joe: He made me happy and supported me physically, intellectually, and spiritually. It took more than money, with which, however, he was most generous, to do so. It took planning and drive and knowledge and the ability to adapt and enjoy other cultures and to meet and befriend new people along the way.

I am thankful also to Joe for leaving me this beautiful place, which I have called home since I was 24. I love every blade of grass, every jonquil, lily, and rose. That weeds, water, emergencies, triumphs, and finding and keeping good renters on the farms are continuing challenges is fine, too. My motto, adopted from an Eastern sage, is

> "Do not try to make things perfect. You may anger the gods."

I hope and believe that Joe would have been happy with what his daughters and I are doing with our lives today. He had faith in us and left us lofty ideals as guides.

GOING ON

Widowhood—1982–1985

How does one learn to cope with living alone after 44 years of marriage?

I will tell you how: One simply has no choice but to carry on. Joe paid me what I felt was a compliment, by naming me his executrix,[1] and the job was such a challenge that I simply had to take hold, to "rise to the occasion," as Mother used to say. So after Joe died, I became a farmer and stayed one for 12 years.

I tackled the hundreds of necessary decisions by following Joe's example and getting advice from persons (mostly also friends) expert in various fields. Richard Cummins had been with Dockery Farms for more than 20 years and knew our land. Debra Machell, who had been here for five years, was also a tower of strength. Lots of people—friends, relatives, staff—helped me get through that year.

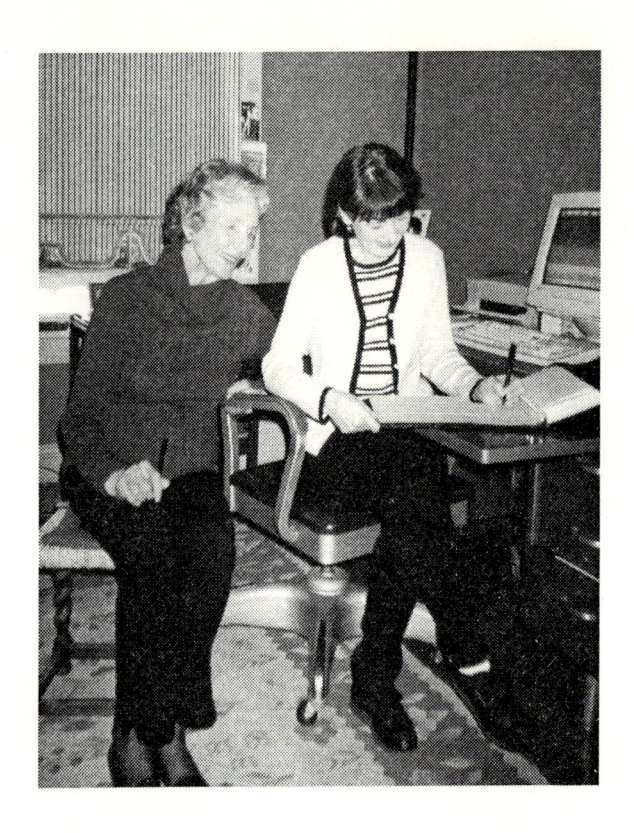

With Debra Machell, without whose help I could not have continued to manage Dockery.

Our daughters were understanding, but Douglas and Kay had their own problems—both were divorced within two years of Joe's death. Though both divorces had been coming for a long time, perhaps Kay and Douglas also wished to spare their father their pain. In addition, the money both inherited may have contributed to their independence. Their needs and my duties turned my thoughts beyond grieving widowhood. I hate the word *widow*—in Spanish *viuda* means both "widow" *and* "empty"—such an ugly sound. Nonetheless, my life was overflowing with problems and duties—settling the estate, deciding to rent the land, and farming itself.

I agree with our farm manager, Steve Brunson, that successful farming is a matter of "drainage, drainage, and drainage."

I have Scotch blood. I'm thrifty. I hate leaving the electricity on.

We made a lot on the first crop of soybeans after Joe died. We planted 5,000 acres for about $150 per acre and sold them at $9 per bushel (They are now worth half that.) While an average yield for the Delta is about 30 bushels per acre, we harvested 40. Thus, we spent $750,000 (plus substantial taxes and investments to improve the soil), and we made over $1,150,000. Soybeans and other commodities have declined in value in spite of inflation. We no longer raise dry land beans; the only money is in irrigated ones. Cotton, which is now low, costs more than $350 an acre to plant. You can't make any money on $5 beans (costing $150 per acre to grow and harvest). It is very expensive to farm—insecticides, fuel, fertilizer, wages, water, land-leveling, equipment, and so on.

It did not seem hard—at that time, anyway—to make money with interest rates in the upper teens.

Joe thought that he left plenty of life insurance money to pay inheritance taxes, and we probated the estate with the help of our auditors and lawyers. We thought everything was done properly, but the courts disagreed.[2] Not until *hours* of work and *seven* years had passed was a settlement reached.

We paid principal and interest to fulfill this judgment until 1997, while operating what the IRS calls a "family farm."

> *I think I did better alone after Joe died than after Hite did. I pulled through my first widowhood well partially because I immediately had so much responsibility and partially because I was ready to give Joe up due to his earlier illnesses. Also, I was 15 years younger.*
>
> *Still, these are the most traumatic of experiences—the loss of two spouses.*

Philanthropy

I don't look upon myself as a significant patron of education and the arts, though I am a founding member of the Ole Miss Women's

Philanthropy Foundation, and I have given parties for and made fairly substantial donations to

- The Center for the Study of Southern Culture
- Delta State
- The Episcopal Church

In addition, after Joe's death, I took his place on the Board of Friends of Mississippi Public Television.

In 1975, with Noel Polk of the University of Southern Mississippi (who became my lifelong friend) and then University of Southern Mississippi President Aubrey Lucas, I was a founding member of the Mississippi Institute of Arts and Letters. With 25 others, I have served as a volunteer board member ever since. We plan programs and find judges willing to serve gratis. The Institute honors with a $1,000 check five or more contemporary Mississippians who are successful and original in the arts—visual (painting, drawing, photography, sculpture), musical composition, and literature (fiction, nonfiction, poetry).

I have gone to all 22 succeeding awards banquets.

Among those honored have been Eudora Welty, Leontyne Price, Walker Percy, Ellen Douglas, Bill Dunlap, and others, including African-American composer William Grant Still (1895–1978).

I knew Still's daughter and granddaughter, who traveled from California to claim for him a posthumous award in 1981.

Voyages On My Own

Santa Fe, 1982

Traveling continued to be a joy even without Joe, though a very different kind of joy. In August I took off for Santa Fe with Great Performance Tours, a New York–based organization. I loved being in that glorious place again, hearing the wonderful music at Santa Fe Opera, meeting new friends. It was the first of several trips I took while living alone.

> *I liked Santa Fe's natural beauty and cultural offerings and the wonderful people who patronize them so much that I've made many more trips back, including three summers in a row after my second widowhood.*

Mexico, 1983

In the winter the year after Joe died, I went back to Acapulco with our friends and neighbors the McCartys, who own a renowned pottery studio near Dockery. Compared to my earlier travels with Joe, Acapulco has become more like Miami Beach. Still, it has some local charm as well as powerboats, sailing, water-skiing, and high-rise apartments. We stayed at Lalo's pensione for 10 days of rest and sunshine—another spot about which I could write at length. Lalo, an elegant Mexican friend of the old school, is a privilege to know.

An African Safari, 1983

The following summer, I packed up three grandchildren between 11 and 12—Elizabeth and Louise Derbes and Will Porteous—and headed for a three-week trip through the Dark Continent via Rome: gelati outside St. Peter's, a picnic at the Villa d'Este, friends on the Via Veneto, sodas atop the Hotel Eden. "This," one of them approved, is "more fun than camp."

A few days later, at midnight, we flew to Nairobi—I with a certain apprehension about taking those valuable travelers into the wild unknown. I wanted to take those three to a new place, one to which none of us had ever been, and Africa certainly qualified. The luxurious Nairobi Hilton was reassuring, the sights fascinating, and communion at All Saint's Cathedral, moving. Will and I roomed together; the girls shared another suite.

For the next 12 days, we criss-crossed Kenya in a Nissan as part of a two-van caravan. We stopped at Amboseli, Outspan, Samburu, Keekorok, and Lake Navasha (flamingos). We saw—quite close—migrating wildebeests and zebras, herds of elephants, prides of lions. We also saw unfamiliar animals—topi, gazelles, impalas, gnu, warthogs. We stayed at the famous Treetop Hotel where young Princess Elizabeth was staying when she learned that her father had died and she had become queen. The rooms were like staterooms on a ship with bunk-beds. From the terrace, we watched the elephants, baboons, monkeys, buffalo, and coyotes that gather at a specially constructed, electrically "moonlit" salt lick by a nearby pond.

The USSR, 1984

> *Dedicated to our wonderful Intourist guide, Yulia Nikiporetz*

Here are some cuttings from my journal's view of a fortnight in the USSR, that is, Mother Russia, (in Russian, *rodina),* with simpatico peers from the South, New England, and New York (that is, *Novgorod* [new town]). Our group of 21 (22, including William Faulkner, whose spirit was always with us) included Southern academics, Mississippi patrons of the arts, Faulkner scholars, and assorted others including my college soulmate from New Orleans, Abby Catledge. Abby was also a recent widow; her husband, *New York Times* editor Turner Catledge, had died the year after Joe did. Abby and I were the survivors of a longstanding close foursome and were glad of each other's presence.

Joe and Hite and I all loved Turner's memoir, *My Life and the Times.* Abby, a flaming liberal, phones me sometimes to talk politics. She says I am her "only real fellow thinker." I shared rooms with Doyce Dees (who became *Doycekaya* by trip's end). For the scholars, the touring was incidental (or was supposed to be incidental) to their main purpose—sharing wisdom with Soviet Faulkner scholars at the Gorky Institute for World Literature with which Ole Miss had been exchanging professors for several years.

For the rest of us, the priorities were reversed. At 69, I was among the oldest; Elizabeth Dalvit, at 25, was the youngest.

The "boys" (in their 40s) were so helpful with little attentions to me, carrying my extra bag, and so on. I think they revere me because of my age, and their deference is touching. I continue to be rich in friends of all ages.

The trip was luxurious, a smooth flight with lovely food (smoked salmon, broiled fish, fresh spinach, fruit, and candy). After our preflight warning from a representative of the International Research and Exchange Board to be circumspect in our dealings with Soviets and talk only of the weather and Faulkner, we were somewhat apprehensive about what lay ahead of this "last supper." The hour and a half of inept customs formalities after 24 hours of traveling was not reassuring. But the warm welcome from our hosts Peter and Sergei, who greeted us with their arms full of peonies, reset the tone. From our hotel—large, modern, severe, no frills—we could see the Kremlin, and some of us walked out late into Red Square to watch the changing of the guards at midnight.

The next day we met with Russian professors at the Gorky Institute, saw films of folk art, landscapes, pottery, and wood carvings, and capped the day with *Giselle,* classic Russian ballet at its best. The next day, we got on the road for a 120-mile bus trip through farmlands and past dachas with bright gardens, many full of lilies. Our destination was Yasnaya Polyana, Tolstoy's home. One high point was viewing the couch on which his wife Anna delivered her *13* children. The following day, we visited the spectacular gold-domed churches flanking Red Square and the Kremlin, and watched tourists file past Lenin's tomb as they have 6 days a week for 60 years. We capped a lovely day by dining on caviar, vodka, and sturgeon with the *New York Times* correspondent, Carl Mydans, and his charming Russian wife, a ballerina. Abby brought us and the Mydans together in one of the most elegant restaurants in the USSR.

For three days, we listened at the Gorky to Russian scholars comparing Faulkner to their great writers like Tolstoy and Dostoevsky. Learned members of our group including Bill Ferris, Noel Polk, Evans

Harrington, Joe Blotner, and Leon Litwak discussed Faulkner in American cultural contexts. After a glittering evening at the American Embassy devoted to Faulkner, we turned the next day back to things Russian and visited a monastery where worshipers' devotions in the face of Soviet disapproval moved me to tears.

Following another lovely dinner, this one a farewell-to-Moscow feast at the House of Composers, we flew Aeroflot to the white nights of Leningrad, where the sun slides to the horizon for only an hour or two just after midnight. In our three days there, we rushed—far too fast—through the treasures of the Hermitage, heard Haydn's *Creation,* and visited the summer home of the czars, the beautifully restored Catherine Palace.

Next—way too soon—we Aeroflotted to Tbilisi, the capital of Georgia, which is at the same latitude as El Paso, Texas. There, the similarity ends. While the scholars conferred with their Georgian counterparts, the rest of us saw museums, tasted wine in caves, and visited a central city market, where our guide put a quick stop to our conversation with a friendly, well-educated Georgian man wishing a chat with the tourists. All of us tasted more lavish Soviet hospitality.

And then on to Moscow to a fancy Fourth-of-July party at the American Embassy featuring the usual caviar and salmon along with charbroiled hamburgers and homemade peach ice cream. Not only the familiar food and drink but also the return to comfortable beds and clean baths were welcome to us spoiled tourists. After the party, many of us wound up our voyage to the USSR with a trip through the rain to a Russian circus. What fun!

The rest of the group went home while I flew alone to fascinating Prague for three days of solo sightseeing. Then, I hopped a train to join relatives in the small Austrian town of Horn. After a flying visit to Vienna, I finally came home again, home again . . .

New York, 1985

In order to keep occupied for the first six months of this auspicious year, I helped to organize a Cleveland group trip to the Metropolitan opera in April. Making that trip particularly lovely was the company of my cousin Coupree Shands and his wife Janet, Frances Patterson, Saralie, Emma, and Marj Haydon.

Notes

[1] Mr. Will Dockery had left the Dockery plantation entailed to his grandchildren. Frances Dockery Cherry, Joe's older sister, got Dockery, and Joe got the Long Lake property. They swapped, and, after Mr. Dockery's death, Joe bought Frances's property for $80,000. Frances had no biological children but had adopted three children, Frances, Kathleen, and Bill Cherry. The federal court of New Orleans ruled that they could not inherit legally from Will, and 2,500 acres bypassed Joe Dockery and Frances Cherry and went to the Dockery daughters. The Cherry children's inheritance came from their parents.

    I still send wedding presents to the Cherry children, and we keep in touch.

[2] All information on the estate is available in the files in the Sunflower County Courthouse, Indianola, and is open to the public.

HITE AGAIN, HITE AGAIN

A Whirlwind Affair

In early March, 1985, the phone rang and at the other end was Hite McLean, a friend from college days at Ole Miss who had written me on the occasion of my engagement to Joe that, under the circumstances, he was going to stop asking me for dates. (See page 67.)

But those had changed! Hite had been a widower since 1983; I, a widow since 1982.

Glad to hear from him, I suggested that he come over to Dockery 10 days later. (I was leaving for New York shortly and explained that I was "really booked up.") Though Hite laughed that I spent most of our first dates explaining how well I was doing on my own, we were happy together from that day until the one on which he died 12 years later. Thoughtful, kind, considerate, and intelligent, Hite, with his superb sense of humor, kept me up, no matter how discouraged I became (and I did become discouraged, mostly about the march of time).

I fell in love with him when I went to his law offices in Greenwood. Hite personified the chivalrous Southern gentleman, the best the Delta could offer, and I didn't even try to resist. But, in spite of his courtly, old-fashioned manners, Hite was ahead of the curve with computers. Having discovered word processing, he retired his secretary and did all his own typing and billing.

Within two months, we were engaged, and within four more, we were married.

Both of us had trips planned and paid for, so we went, separately. Hite went with his cousins to Scotland; my daughter Keith and I went to San Francisco to see Wagner's *Ring*.

Hite and I had such fun. We went out to eat. I took him to several charity events. I was singing the Mozart *Requiem* in the choral group at Delta State, and Hite brought his daughter Kim and son-in-law Jim Spencer to listen. Hite just fit in my lifestyle.

We were both on the fast track.

"My passport's ready," he'd say. "When do we leave?"

We had a complete division of finances, often the basis of a real good marriage, young or old.

There are some virtues of marriages between the elderly: Usually people have enough wherewithal, and you don't have to worry about getting pregnant.

Hite said to me once, "I wish we could have a baby." Such a sweet thing to say.

Our families blended beautifully: Hite had four grandchildren; I had seven, then six, when my grandson Gail Clark died.

When Hite and I became engaged, we had to have some counseling. We went to see Lee Belford, a retired Episcopal priest and a charming man.

Lee offered us a drink, and we sat around talking. "What can I tell you two, married 44 years and 46 years?" We became fast friends.

I also went to a clinic near San Antonio for counseling right before the wedding. You'd be interviewed by a therapist alone, and then you'd go into a group and discuss everyone's problems together. It was great—I recommend it for anyone who can afford it.

Carolyn Lee Clark
Thomas Gail Clark, III
Elizabeth Keith Derbes
Ann Louise Derbes
Alison Corinne Derbes
Will Dockery Porteous
Alexandra Keith Porteous

James Luther Spencer, IV
Hite McLean Spencer
Mathilde Overton McLean
George Hite McLean, IV

have the joy of announcing
the marriage
of their grandparents

Keith Somerville Dockery
and
George Hite McLean

on the fifteenth of July
one thousand nine hundred and eighty-five
St. John's Episcopal Church
Memphis, Tennessee

They announced our marriage.

The same year I married Hite, Douglas married Wilmer Thomas. Hite and I married in a family-members-only ceremony at St. John's Episcopal Church in Memphis on July 15, 1985, with John Brewster officiating. Our five children and seven grandchildren attended, and our grandsons Hite Spencer and Gail Clark read the lessons.

Hite's brother Lee and his wife Stella were there. So were my sister Ashton and nephew "young George" (in his early 40s).

July 14, 1985—Hite and me on our wedding day.

That we could share our joy with Ashton became especially precious when cancer took her four months later.

Ashton and me on my wedding day.

Our wonderful reception and supper was held at the Memphis Polo Club for 50 people with a great jazz pianist. Ashton and Douglas did the flowers. We danced and feasted until late in the evening.

Hite Junior drove us to the Peabody Hotel, where we spent the night. The next day, we drove to the Red Apple Inn in Arkansas for a short honeymoon.

Our Green Salad Days

Hite moved in with me at Dockery where we fashioned a wonderful life for each other. We changed the master bedroom from the front to the rear of the hall; otherwise Dockery remained pretty much the same as it had been since I was in my 50s.

Hite commuted to Greenwood each day for his law practice but managed to be free to travel with his gypsy wife when—as was frequent—I wished. I continued to look to Dockery's farming interests, which occupied lots of time and thoughts but left me free to do as I pleased when I pleased, a great privilege.

> *In college, Hite was young-looking, and we wondered, "Is he ever going to grow up?"*
>
> *Obviously, he did.*
>
> *He married Lenore Kimbrough, a beautiful lady, whose wonderful children called her "Momma." She eventually went back to school at Delta State, earned a teaching certificate, and taught grammar school for several years.*
>
> *She died when her pacemaker failed in 1983.*
>
> *Hite and Lenore had two children—Kim and Hite Junior—four grandchildren, and three great-grandchildren.*

Hite was a happy, fun person but at the same time very intellectual. He loved historical novels like Kenneth Roberts's *Northwest Passage*, which he read and reread. His legal background was impeccable. Like Atticus in *To Kill a Mockingbird*, he loved the law—it was his life. He reminded some of my friends of Faulkner's

Gavin Stevens, the wise lawyer in the Snopes' trilogy who many think was Faulkner's mouthpiece.

Once he asked, rhetorically, "Isn't it fun being a lawyer?"

"I think it's the most boring thing I've ever encountered," I replied.

He had an eclectic taste in literature—biography, history, humor, not so much the classics. Hite found *The Piano* pornographic, and he was a Republican, bringing Oliver North propaganda home to tease me, but we laughed away our differences.

Hite entertains our mutual friend Faulkner biographer Joe Blotner.

In fall of 1986, Hite and I co-hosted (with 11 others) a three-day-long fall cotton festival in the Delta for 50 friends and neighbors. The event coincided with the board meeting of the Center for the Study of Southern Culture, promoted volunteerism, and raised funds for the Center. We kicked events off with a dinner party at a co-host's plantation followed by music and a surprise guest, Center Director Bill Ferris. The next morning, celebrants had a choice of tours of Stapl Cotn Cooperative, in business since 1920, or Cottonlandia, a regional museum, and took care of business in a meeting before lunch, which was served in the gardens of a cohost's plantation. The wines came from vineyards at nearby Indianola, a locale not, unfortunately, noted for its fine grapes.

Then, we all piled into cars and drove through fields of cotton and soybeans as well as rice paddies and catfish ponds to Carrollton for wine and sandwiches at Jess Pinkston's Woodston Hall (1841). Back at Greenwood that night, many of us enjoyed a live production of *My Fair Lady*. The festivities ended with lunch at a contemporary home with a wonderful Delta view.

Sometime in the early 1990s, the son of an old friend stayed several days with Hite and me. We both loved this young man, and I will always miss his gentle presence and steadfast friendship. He was gay and tried unsuccessfully to overcome his nature. His parents never accepted his homosexuality. He built a beautiful career as an architect but became enamored of a botany professor who died. Brokenhearted, he moved in with his brother and tried—again unsuccessfully—to make amends with his father and mother. His desire to become an Episcopal priest was thwarted because at that point, the church was not accepting homosexual clergy, and one sad day, he shot himself fatally. He was only in his early 50s. He left a note: "This is not a murder; it is a suicide."

I had a sense when I was at Ole Miss of several guys who were kind of different from other men. They seemed effeminate, tended to have queer, prissy walks, and often majored in the arts. At that time, they tended to choose to stay apart from mainstream campus life, or so I guessed, anyhow. Since then, of course, I've learned of the honored place homosexuals held in the Greek world of Aristotle and Plato. And now many people I know and admire are openly gay.

Travels with Hite

Italy, 1986

Our honeymoon was brief, so we made up time with a leisurely three weeks abroad early the next year in Italy, Switzerland, and France. Landing in Napoli, we rented a car and headed down the

Amalfi drive and drove inland to snowy Ravello, atop of one of the coast's mountains, where we wandered in the gardens where Wagner composed *Tristan and Isolde*. Together we walked and looked, looked and walked. Hite loved everything, even the funny European elevators set into ancient stairwells.

Then we doubled back to Rome, where we passed a long and fascinating day with Joe and Yvonne Blotner, whom I'd met on the Faulkner tour of the USSR two years earlier. We drove together to Hadrian's villa (second century AD) outside Rome for a lovely day of sightseeing. Hadrian had been as much of a tourist as we and considerably more of an architect—the designs for the villa were entirely his, and he named parts of it for places he had loved on his travels in pursuit of his imperial duties. The four of us spent hours wandering around the "villa"—many buildings actually, set beautifully into the Roman countryside. Hite and I loved both Joe and Yvonne, and we were deeply saddened by her death a few years after our Roman holiday. When Joe married Marnie Allen, who has also become a close friend, he told Hite and me that it was the example of our happiness that gave him the nerve to dare remarriage, and we three still visit back and forth between Dockery and Joe's retirement post in Charlottesville, Virginia.

Entering the beautiful Renaissance Duomo on a rainy day in Florence, Hite and I were shocked back into the present by the headline about the Challenger tragedy. So sad—All those young lives gone in an instant explosion in the sky.

Leaving Italy, the train from Florence to Switzerland was marooned in a snowstorm in the Swiss Alps. The stop added a few hours of excitement to our trip and offered more opportunities to meet interesting fellow travelers. We spent two brief but rewarding days sightseeing in Lucerne, especially loving the covered bridges. We also enjoyed the *train de grande vitesse*, which we took to Burgundy.

There, I introduced Hite to Joe's and my longtime friends the Chevignards, as well as the Lescure clan, including Michel and his wife Chantal Mazy-Perrier. Michel's Peugeot flew us down the highways at speeds almost equivalent to the train—No *limites de vitesse* on French highways—to the Chalet in Nuits St. Georges. As we sped along, to show off his car, Michel flung open a door. "Fermez la porte," said the computer in his car severely, sending us into gales of laughter.

Both families included marvelous chefs. When Chantal blew a hunting horn to announce dinner, we gathered and dined sumptuously, chatting happily and intimately. Hite fit in instantly, and our admiration and pleasure were mutual.

The People's Republic of China, 1987

Our fellow travelers, members of the United States—China People's Friendship Association, were mostly well prepared and intelligent, eager to get to know new people in a strange land, and helpful to each other. Our expedition, framed by some delightful days in San Francisco, was significantly enriched by the wisdom of Cecilia Lin (a Memphis artist of Taiwanese heritage who served as our tour guide). Of many adventures, we especially enjoyed two boat excursions, one on the Li River from Guilin, whose unadorned natural beauty is, I think, unsurpassed, and another on the Yangtze.

Tourist facilities—especially toilet-free buses and alcohol-free airplanes—were sometimes dismaying, but in general we lived graciously and were sumptuously feted by our Chinese hosts. As always, Hite and I made new friends among our travel group—Angelinos Pat and Chris Weil and Dick and Phyllis Hicks, with whom I keep in touch. We also met Cha Fu-chi through a Chinese friend of a longtime friend of Aunt Lucy's. Fu-chi, who was waiting for us at the lovely JinLing Hotel in Nanjing, accompanied us on a two-day sightseeing journey to see the Ming Tombs 30 miles northeast of Beijing where 13 emperors of the Ming dynasty (1368–1644) and their empresses and concubines are buried. On this trip, we also stopped at the Great Wall, which entailed a fairly stiff climb. Chris Weil endeared himself to me by carrying me up on his back.

When we learned that Fu-chi was coming to the States later in the fall, we invited him to visit us at Dockery and arranged a speaking engagement for him at Delta State. His talk on Taoism as religion and as philosophy was warmly received, and he returned to us several times. He had hoped to attend Ole Miss or a university in New Orleans in Southern Studies, but neither Steve Derbes nor I could arrange the necessary financial assistance. After earning an advanced degree in teaching English as a second language at the University of Illinois at Urbana-Champaign, he was joined by his 16-year-old son and his wife. He now teaches at Columbia University in New York City, where I recently saw all three of them.

I have seldom entertained house guests with manners as elegant as Fu-chi and his friends, including Dazhuanf Ye and Zhuang Jun, two young students who were among the survivors of the Tiananmen Square Massacre in Beijing in June 1989. A year later at Dockery, they cooked wonderful Chinese food for us, and in return I made cornbread for them.

Wrote Fu-chi in his thank you note: "We are really good cooks. You seemed to enjoy it simply it had so different flavor from yours," concluding by wishing us "happiness, health, and longevity." His friend Zhuang wrote sweetly that he was scarcely able to tear himself "from you and the love atmosphere of your family," while Dazhuanf wrote that the photos we sent helped him remember the "unforgettable very nice days during our visit."

It was awe-inspiring to have them at our table.

So much has happened in China since then.

Back in the USSR, 1988

While we were officially in the Soviet Union for a legal seminar (which Hite attended religiously), the trip was by no means all work and no play. It couldn't be since Hite thought the idea up, and, when the tour was being organized, encouraged his law professor, John Marshall, to lead it. John had been a stunningly young professor when he was teaching Hite at Ole Miss; now he was a very old man, teaching at Vanderbilt.

Hite also came up with the excellent idea that we take with us our three 11-year-old granddaughters Keith Porteous, Alison Derbes, and Mathilde McLean. The girls were the hit of that group, who enjoyed them almost as much as we did. In those Cold War days, we were lucky to manage some person-to-person contact with the Russian people. Young girls' smiles and waves do wonders in destroying language barriers.

I wish they had kept the journals I'd requested, so I could include their fresh views here.

Granddaughters abroad—Keith Porteous, Alison Derbes, Mathilde McLean (1988).

We swam in the Black Sea at Odessa and waded in the Baltic at Leningrad (now St. Petersburg). The gigantic rather poorly run hotels in the USSR didn't bother the girls at all. All among our mostly charming fellow travelers, in fact, were good tourists and good sports.

We celebrated our third wedding anniversary at Pyatigorsk, a spa near Tbilisi, Georgia. The girls did the planning, having brought favors and balloons from home and gathering wild flowers from the adjoining woods. The hotel supplied champagne, and we dined buffet-style in its spacious dining room atop a tier of concrete steps leading down to beautiful gardens and a rippling fountain. Hite and I danced together, and then he danced with each of the girls. We had a grand time: Like all our anniversaries, this one was memorable and happy.

Then on to white nights in Leningrad (now St. Petersburg to most but not to me), a city resplendent with tuberous begonias.

And, finally, the road homeward.

Greece, 1994

We met Hite's brother and wife on a cruise and then took a three-day bus ride with a couple from Ole Miss on what the tourist agency called the "classic tour." I just love Greece.

We went swimming in the Aegean, wandering in ruins from Archaic and Classical Greece, eating tomatoes and seafood, drinking good local wines.

> *It's fabulous, being able to live on my memories. I'm lucky, very lucky.*

South America, 1997

Hite had never been to South America, and he came home one day carrying an ad for a cruise organized by Harvard University and guided by an anthropologist. "We might want to do this," he suggested, and shortly thereafter we flew to Buenos Aires, where we boarded the Odysseus for a trip around Cape Horn and through the Straits of Magellan. The South American fiords apparently compare to those in Scandinavia. We loved our fellow travelers (many of them Ivy League professors), the food, the dancing (though Hite was slowing down), and the marvelous lectures from people as knowledgeable as the former ambassador to Argentina. Hite was a splendid companion because of his stunning ability to make friends.

> *My last trip with both my husbands was to South America. Fate?*

Back on the Home Front

Life was pleasant, fun, settled. After Hite left for work, I'd do a little bit of gardening and a lot of picking and arranging of flowers. There were errands to be run, friends, relatives, and acquaintances to visit, books to be read, courses and lectures to attend at Delta State. We had frequent house guests. And I continued active in church, community, and art circles. Dockery takes a lot of tending. I officially retired as manager of Dockery in 1994, but there was still a lot of work to be done.

Hite and I went to church Sundays and entertained frequently at Dockery, his friends from Greenwood or mine from Cleveland. They quickly became "ours." Hite loved his lawyering, and he drove the 38 miles to Greenwood Monday through Fridays to his law offices, a quick trip with only one stoplight between us. Both of us continued active in civic and community affairs. Hite was a prominent part of the law community. He had been president of the Leflore County Bar Association and, as attorney for the Leflore County School Board comprising two token whites and six blacks, had been intimately involved in all the segregation battles of the last 30 years. Like most Greenwood whites, Hite grew up a staunch segregationist, but, after working with the members of the school board, came full circle to support integration and the Civil Rights movement wholeheartedly. Hite's evolving attitude was like that of many other white Southerners.

Friends and colleagues valued him for his courtesy, his wit, his sharp mind, and his respect for varying positions. Said one colleague, a lawyer, "He had a very recognizable laugh. If you heard it, you knew he was in the building." The superintendent of the Leflore county schools, who like most of the other members of the Board was black, characterized Hite as "the epitome of the gentleman lawyer. I think he practiced law with a great deal of civility, which is the exception rather than the rule now." The superintendent went on to quote Hite, "Every problem has within itself the seeds of its own solution." That sentence captures for me the essence of Hite's gentle and practical approach not only to the law but also to life itself.

Hite was home by 4:30 or 5:30. Then, he sometimes went to see his daughter, Kim Spencer, who was then teaching writing at Delta State, and her husband, Jim. (We saw a lot of our children, and they seemed to heartily approve their parents' match, although we only rarely shared political consensus.)

> *Hite Junior, has been particularly sweet, remembering me with flowers on special occasions like anniversaries, birthdays, and Valentine's Day. My affection for all of Hite and Lenore's children and their children is boundless.*

Hite and I started weekday evenings with the *NewsHour*, sometimes cocktail in hand, sometimes not. Then, we ate dinner, which I usually cooked—Hite was not much of a cook. Evenings, we didn't much go to the movies or watch many sporting events, preferring to stay home and read. I'm omnivorous; Hite was too. His particular favorite, however, was David McCulloch. Often, we'd take a walk after dinner, before Hite's breathing problems slowed our pace. We'd go back through the Dockery gate and across highway 8 to the old black cemetery.

Friday was a special night, calling for a martini for Hite and a vermini for me (reversed proportions gin and vermouth). Saturday mornings at 10, Hite often went to see Kim and Jim, stopping on the way back to get us something for lunch.

Sometimes we went to parties in Cleveland or neighboring towns; sometimes we gave them. As our friends got older and many became reluctant to drive at night, we had lots of company here overnight.

Me and my helpers—Debby Fort, my cousin and editor, and Cathy Jones, my invaluable girl Friday.

We did travel a whole lot both abroad and at home, almost always with friends or relations the ultimate reason for our journeys.

I was proud to be part of the promotion of the *Encyclopedia of Southern Culture* in the offices of the U.S. Senate. Along with other members of a large delegation from the board of the Center, we flew to Washington, D.C., to celebrate its publication at a huge reception in the Senate Office Building. We ate moon pies and Mississippi catfish, and the open bar featured mint juleps and bourbon and branch water.

In 1994, the governor and the Mississippi Arts Commission gave me a "Governor's Award for Excellence in the Arts."

Aunt Lucy and Dockery had a banner year in 1995. They both turned 100. (Mr. Will Dockery came here in 1895; Joe Rice was born in 1906; I'd been here since 1938.) Hite and I and my daughters held a centennial in July attended by 90 members of four generations of Dockerys, Somervilles, and Fraziers, Forts, and their in-laws, especially including the McLeans. They came from as far away as Ethiopia (where Ashton's daughter Ashton Douglass and her family were living).

Here are as many of us as will fit in the photo taken at the Cleveland ceremony honoring Aunt Lucy.

Most of us gathered at Crawdad's, a popular, fun country café in Merigold for a festive dutch treat Friday night.

Sunday's focus was on Aunt Lucy, beginning in the afternoon with a beautiful reception at the Cleveland Country Club. Dorothy Shawhan, who had already immortalized Lucy in a character *à clef* in her recent novel *Lizzie* and who is currently at work on Aunt Lucy's biography, was the primary speaker.

> *Aunt Lucy remained gracious, enthusiastic, an inspiration to us all.*

I loved the whole celebration, but I also loved its prequel, an early morning hot-air balloon ride. I'd never been up in a balloon basket before, and it is exciting. After the country club celebration was over, we moved on to Dockery for a catfish fry accompanied by a three-piece combo—sometimes a quartet when I joined at the piano, an upright in the pool house which had belonged to Miss Helen, Hite's mother, and on which she had once taught children to play. Hite, our children, and our grandchildren sang.

Keith Somerville Dockery McLean

Visiting Our Offspring

Hite and I loved seeing them all. We visited

- Douglas and Wilmer at their grand New York apartment and new home in Connecticut.
- Kay and Gail at their pretty home in Tulsa. Gail was an especially graceful, thoughtful host, helping us in every way he could to enjoy ourselves.

Thomas Gail Clark (1966–1990)

Born in Oklahoma, Kay and Tom's second child was a darling little boy with great promise. Brown-eyed and dark-haired, Gail had a quick mind, and great determination and courage. But he did not begin to walk at two and he could not run without falling. We all worried. When Gail was five, we learned to our heartbreak that he had muscular dystrophy—Duchenne's—the worst kind.

Kay and Tom tended him together until their divorce in 1983; after that Kay devoted her life to caring for her son.

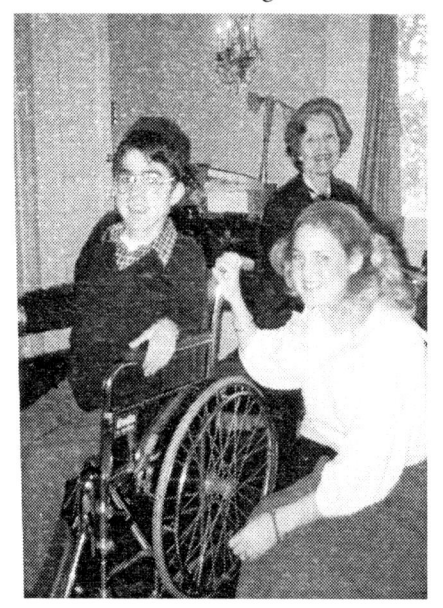

Kay's children, Caroline and Gail Clark, and me.

> Gail was an inspiration to us all. He studied faithfully and persistently, graduating from elementary and high school and going on to Tulsa Junior College. He was knowledgeable about sports, attending many matches in person and watching others on TV.
>
> Shortly before Gail died, Hite and I put him and Kay on a plane in Florida to fly to his sister's wedding on the West Coast. Excited, he looked up at me from his wheel chair and promised, "See you in California!" What spunk!
>
> Our lives were enriched by his uncomplaining bravery and his valiant spirit.
>
> We miss him.

- All the Derbes, in the joyful, relaxed atmosphere of their New Orleans home, welcoming so many drop-in friends for late-night sessions singing along to tunes from my old piano, now restored and active again. We also got together in the mountains of Tennessee and on the beaches of Florida.
- Kim and Jim Spencer, Hite's daughter and son-in-law, first in Cleveland and then in Greenwood. I remember especially warmly a Christmas Eve party in Memphis.
- Hite Junior and his lovely, independent wife, Virginia Overton McLean, in Memphis. Hite Junior is a great reader with whom I still exchange books. He reads late every night, and I have some trouble keeping up with him

And Our Offspring Visiting Us

Our daughters, their spouses, our grandchildren, great-grandchildren (!), and Hite's children and children's children have come frequently to Dockery over the years. While each visit and visitor is unique, we usually shared several communal activities. Generations have toasted marshmallows before cheerful fires in the Dockery living room fireplace. And often we have family "read-alouds." All my daughters and their children learned to swim in the Dockery pool. At dinnertime, we gathered around a dining-room table set with silver and china and always bearing fresh flowers. I arranged roses, zinnias, jonquils, iris, depending on the season, hothouse flowers in the winter. As dusk fell, we lit the candles. Often, during the long summers, we dined al fresco on the patio or by the pool. Other times, we piled into the car for fried fish and other delicacies at a nearby restaurant. Almost every visit called for a trip to the McCarty's pottery, both to greet our old friends and, usually, to make purchases as well.

Mostly our times together are unalloyed joys, but some are bittersweet now. During evening sing-alongs around the piano that Joe gave me, for example, I miss both Hite and Joe especially sharply.

TWICE A WIDOW

Hite died of emphysema in 1997, 30 years after he had quit smoking. During his last couple of months, I had wonderful help from Cathy Jones at home, who has, thank God, stayed on with me. Eventually my faith was strengthened, and I came to accept this second grievous loss, but there were some hard hard times along the way.

I got quality points with Hite's children when he asked me from his hospital bed, "Keith, make it easy. Give me the easy way."

I took out the oxygen tubes and asked no one specific: "Dr. Kevorkian, where are you now when we need you so?"

The attending doctor gave Hite a shot, Hite's breathing became easier, and he was gone. George Hite McLean (April 2, 1917–August 1, 1997) was buried in Winona, Mississippi. The Reverend Lee Winter conducted the funeral.

I think of Hite and Joe when they were healthy and vital, not as sick old men in hospital beds.

After Hite died, I became more and more insecure. I was afraid I'd go out and have a wreck. I was afraid of death. So I went to see Dr. Ted Lathram, who'd recently retired at 82 and who'd helped Joe years back. He said I was "the best-adjusted patient" he'd ever had. Thank God for the computer and Prozac.

Solo Again

I get restless when I've been away too long, and I want to be back home at Dockery. It's fun traveling alone, however. Mother traveled until her 85th birthday, and I'm still on the road at 86. It's great when you get to 75 or so. You can do what you want to. You have freedom.

To keep fit, I *try* to ride a stationary bicycle three times a week for about 10 minutes, and I always do calisthenics for 10 to12 minutes, plus walking and swimming.

On Easter night in the late 1990s, the black Baptist church on Dockery burned. I've always wondered if the fire had been set by vigilantes, though that has never been proved. It supposedly caught fire from faulty wiring; if it were a hate crime, that would make its loss even sadder. Although we invited the parishioners to rebuild at Dockery, they chose to locate their new church at Ruleville.

In the last year of the 20th century, I was made an "ageless hero" [*sic*] by Blue Cross/Blue Shield. Creativity is expressed not just in the arts. It should apply generally—cooking, gardening, flower-arranging, everything. Osceola McCarty, who died this year at 91, had been similarly honored by the Blues earlier.

Truly An Aged Heroine

Osceola McCarty took in laundry from age 13 to age 88, after leaving school in sixth grade to help support her family. As "just a little old colored woman who walked everywhere," she saved her earnings and in 1996 gave $150,000 to the University of Southern Mississippi in Hattiesburg, her birthplace, for the education of young blacks. Her philosophy is summarized in her book *Simple Wisdom for Rich Living*. She received the Presidential Citizens Medal, the Wallenberg Humanitarian Award, the Avicenna Medal from UNESCO, and an honorary doctorate of humane letters from Harvard.

In January, I got a snazzy new Gateway computer with Windows 98. I hired a number of computer teachers, and, slowly, I'm mastering it. It's a whole new world.

I'll be damned! This is *fascinating*.

I love e-mail. Getting an e-mail from my granddaughter Alison Derbes written in a cybercafe in the Bangkok airport—what fun!

Early in the new millennium, I drove to Ole Miss for a meeting of the executive board of the Center for the Study of Southern Culture (comprising 25 people culled from the 100 regular members). I am pleased at the splendid job Charlie Wilson and Ann Abadie are doing. Bill Ferris's[1] shoes are not easy to fill, but Ann and Charlie are doing well.

There are some good things about growing old. You can flirt shamelessly with younger men without getting rebuked.

Unfortunately, there are plenty of bad ones as well. In early spring of 2000, I tripped in a dark parking lot and broke my right wrist, an injury which my friend Terry Simmons said I handled with "panache." I don't know, but I hated being unable to drive for six weeks and having to depend hard on my wonderful helper Cathy Jones's expert care, both nursing me and around the house. Although I had to cancel my trip with Keith and Debby Fort to Oxford for the annual Conference on the Book, I was back in harness by May, traveling to Natchez with Terry and Saralie and Mississippi Public Radio administrator and longtime friend William Fulton to attend the opera. And my wrist seems perfectly healed now.

Friendships lasting a lifetime: Saralie, Emma, and me.

With others, I worked to keep the state from widening the road, cutting both into Dockery and the black cemetery on the grounds which would be a tragedy for us all. With my friends and neighbors, the local media, representatives from the State Archives, and faculty from Delta State's history department, we won this battle in August 2000.

In 2001, I was proud to be honored with the Gladys Castle Friend of Delta State award for service by a nonalumna. I was 10 when Delta State was founded, with help from Daddy and the Howorths, and I have grown old with it.

Baptism near Perthshire, my favorite painting in Emma's Retrospective.

Later that spring, my daughter Keith and I packed our bags and flew to Italy for two weeks. We spent a week in Rome in the apartment cousin Keith Fort and his wife Debby had rented in the beautiful Campo dei Fiori.

Keiths left to right: Fort, McLean, Derbes.

Almost everything but St. Peter's was within easy walking distance; Rome was at its balmy springtime best in centuries. In honor of last year's Jubilee, Pope John Paul II had spruced up the city in general and opened many buildings and churches closed for decades. Seeing the excavations under the Vatican and the Bernini sculptures in the Galleria Borghese, open for the first time in 15 years, was especially wonderful.

We ate like royalty, not only from the bounty of the Campo dei Fiori and the paneficio and salsamentaria in our neighborhood, but also at many terrific restaurants, for not very much money. Unlike here, the wine part of the meal, a major part of the pleasure, was always an insubstantial part of the bill. Truffles and artichokes were in season. Need I say more?

Our Roman holiday was further enriched when Keith and Debby's friend Franco Antonelli came to call and kept us under his wing for the rest of the stay. Franco was the fiancé of a friend of Debby's about 40 years ago. The union ultimately collapsed when it became clear that Mama, cross, Catholic, and shrouded, would always have to live with them. Franco took the four of us—three Keiths and a Debby—out to a marvelous dinner in the Castelli Romani, doing all the ordering off the menu, drowning us in fabulous food, and insisting on paying.

Daughter Keith and I then met Louise and Steve Derbes in Fiesole for a lovely long weekend there and in Florence before we returned briefly to Rome and flew home.

Barely was I unpacked before Saralie and I set off for a month of opera and culture in Santa Fe, meeting acquaintances who had become friends and making new ones. This was the third summer in a row (1999–2001) that the two of us made that pilgrimage, spending the first of our two-week stints attending St. John's College Summer Classics offerings. Those first years, we stayed at a hotel quite near the main town square, convenient to the college. Once you get used to it, the 7,000-foot altitude seemed energizing not debilitating. While Saralie had a bit more trouble acclimatizing than I did, we both had to decompress each time when we returned home to hot Mississippi air at a mere 300 feet above sea level.

The intellectual climate in Santa Fe is as bracing at the altitude and as arresting as its amazing vistas. In that unbelievable scenery thrive 250 art galleries (or so I was told) as well as many musical offerings—opera, concerts, chamber music, the Desert Chorale, and more. In addition there were lectures and seminars at the college. Classes examining various facets of opera taught by Director of Mississippi Public Radio William Fulton were our main academic focus in 2001. We studied *Mitridate, Ré di Ponto* Mozart's composition at age 14 (!); *Lucia di Lammermoor;* and *The Egyptian Helen,* a wonderful if obscure opera by Richard Strauss.

We had such a fine time in Santa Fe that we decided to increase our stay to a month. Through the connections of my old friend Pimmie Tucker and her daughter, we were able to rent a house—well, parts of a house—overlooking the gorgeous expanse of desert and mountains which is greater Santa Fe. The views, breathtaking in several directions, were constant sources of joy and inspiration. Our hostess, a young lawyer in a firm that helps Native American victims of abuse, was away most of the time and generously invited Saralie and me to enjoy the run of the house.

She even encouraged us to hold a party in her home, so of course we did. On July 14, we invited about 20 friends wearing red, white, and blue to celebrate Bastille Day. We hobnobbed with returnees from past years, new and old friends from elsewhere, and the Santa Fe natives we've been lucky enough to meet. We particularly enjoyed the company of five attractive young women from Cleveland vacationing in the area for five days.

Our social life this year as before continued *très gai*.

Nonetheless, at times, I am terribly, terribly lonely.

I fight this feeling. I want to keep in touch with everybody. Then you get close to so many people. I don't just accept—I respond. I look up distant relatives, and often they don't stay distant. I seek out friends of friends, and they become friends of mine as well. My circle is ever widening, and that's how I like it.

I am such a lucky lady.

Safe at Dockery.

Note

[1] After 20 years as Center director, Bill Ferris took a leave of absence in 1998 to head the National Endowment for the Humanities in Washington, D.C. He is now professor of history and associate director of the University of North Carolina's' Center for the Study of the American South.

APPENDIXES

My grandchildren surround me (except for Carolyn Clark Powers who could not be in New Orleans on Christmas, 2000). From left to right: Louise Derbes, Elizabeth Derbes, Keith Porteous, Elizabeth Porteous, me, Will Dockery Porteous, Alison Derbes. I hope next year's card will feature my four *great* grandchildren!

Carolyn and Bill Powers and their extended family.

Appendix 1: The Dockery Daughters

Daughters	Keith Douglas (**Douglas**), my first-born, has drive—some inherited, yes, but a lot in her shaping of what her environment offers. She and I have much in common. 1-7-41	Hughla McKay (**Kay**), my middle child, was the early on less assertive than her sisters. She was very social with her peers. She once told me that her proudest day had been her high school graduation, and I am now so proud to see her graduate from college in her early 50s. 10-31-42	Mary Keith (**Keith**) was the baby. Everybody always loved her. She was a curly-haired little girl, always sweet and happy. She never seemed to feel dominated by her older sisters, becoming her own person early on. 11-23-44
High School	St. Anne's Episcopal School, Charlottesville, Virginia, one year; graduated Lausanne School for Girls, Memphis 1958	Graduated Lausanne, 1960	Graduated Lausanne, 1962
College	Sweetbriar College 1962 BA Phi Beta Kappa, Indiana University (Teaching certificate)	Oklahoma University, 1960–1962; University of Memphis, 1996, BA	Mills College (California), 1962—1964 Newcomb College, 1966, BA; St. Nicholas Training Center For Montessori Education (London) 1967 (Teaching Certificate)
Marriage	William Alexander Porteous III (**Bill**) 1969 (divorced, 1983) Wilmer J. Thomas, 1985	Thomas Gail Clark, 1961 (divorced, 1983)	Stephen Joseph Derbes, MD, 1967
Grandchildren	William Dockery Porteous (**Will**), 1972, m. Elizabeth Diane Neumann 1997. Alexandra Keith Porteous (**Keith**), 1977	Carolyn Lee Clark, 1962 m. John Creator, 1988 (divorced, 1999) m. William Powers (**Bill**), 1999 Thomas Gail Clark (**Gail**), 1966–1990.	Elizabeth Keith Derbes Elizabeth, 1970 Anne Louise Derbes (**Louise**), 1971 Alison Corinne Derbes (**Alison**), 1977
Great Grandchildren	Isobel Douglas Porteous (2001)	John Roy, Cleator (**Johnny**),1989 Thomas Gail Cleator (**Tom**), 1991 William Clark Dockery Powers, 2000	

Appendix 2: The Grandchildren Set Forth

A rich whirl of—naturally!—brilliant grandchildren. Here are some high points, but along the way, we made various side trips for grandparents' days and elementary school and high school graduations and other special events.

	Elementary School
Trinity Episcopal School, New Orleans	*Elementary schools nationwide*
Elizabeth Derbes (1984), First in Class	James Luther Spencer, IV (Jay)
Louise Derbes (1985)	Hite McLean Spencer
Will Porteous (1986)	*Hutchinson School, Memphis*
Keith Porteous (1991)	Mathilde Overton McLean
Alison Derbes (1992), First in Class	*Memphis University School*
Grimes Elementary School, Tulsa, Oklahoma	George Hite McLean, IV
Gail Clark	
Carolyn Clark	
	High School
Memorial High School, Tulsa, Oklahoma	*The Hill School, Pottstown, Pennsylvania*
Carolyn Clark (1981)	Jay Spencer (1984)
Bishop Kelly High School Tulsa, Oklahoma	Hite Spencer (1987)
Gail Clark (1985)	*St. Mary's Episcopal School, Memphis*
The Taft School, Watertown, Connecticut	Mathilde McLean (1996)
Elizabeth Derbes (1988), Valedictorian	*Uppingham School (UK)*
Louise Derbes (1989)	Jay Spencer (1985)
Will Porteous (1990)	*Memphis University School*
St. Paul's School, Concord, New Hampshire	Hite McLean
Keith Porteous (1995)	
Phillips Academy, Andover, Massachusetts	
Alison Derbes (1996)	
	University
University of Oklahoma, Norman	*Vanderbilt University, Tennessee*
Carolyn Clark (1985)	Jay Spencer (1989)
Tulsa Junior College, Oklahoma	Hite Spencer (1991)
Gail Clark	*Dartmouth College, New Hampshire*
Harvard University, Cambridge	Mathilde McLean (2000)
Elizabeth Derbes (1992), Magna Cum Laude	
Georgetown University, Washington, D.C.	
Louise Derbes (1993), Cum Laude	
Stanford University, Palo Alto, California	
Will Porteous (1994)	
Princeton University, New Jersey	
Keith Porteous (1999)	
Alison Derbes (2000)	

	Postgraduate
Antioch College, California	*Vanderbilt University*
Carolyn Clark (1998), MS	Jay Spencer (1989), MS Engineering
University of Chicago School of Law	Hite Spencer (1992) MS Engineering
Elizabeth Derbes (1998) with honors	
INSEAD, Fontainebleau, France	
Louise Derbes (1998), MBA	
Harvard University, Cambridge	
Will Porteous (2000), MBA	

BVG